D0679651

DELPHI PUBLIC LIBRARY

222 East Main Street

Delphi, Indiana 46923

765-564-2929

Two Histories of England

Two Histories of England

By
Jane Austen
and
Charles Dickens

Introduced by
David Starkey

ecco

An *Imprint of* HarperCollins*Publishers*

TWO HISTORIES OF ENGLAND. Copyright © 2006 by Icon Books Ltd. Introduction copyright © 2006 by David Starkey. All rights reserved. Printed in the United States of America. No part of this book may be used or reproduced in any manner whatsoever without written permission except in the case of brief quotations embodied in critical articles and reviews. For information address HarperCollins Publishers, 10 East 53rd Street, New York, NY 10022.

HarperCollins books may be purchased for educational, business, or sales promotional use. For information please write: Special Markets Department, HarperCollins Publishers, 10 East 53rd Street, New York, NY 10022.

Jane Austen's *The History of England* originally written in 1791. Charles Dickens's *A Child's History of England* originally published in 1851–1853.

This edition first published in Great Britain in 2006 as *The History of England* by Icon Books Ltd.

FIRST U.S. EDITION

Library of Congress Cataloging-in-Publication Data is available upon request.

ISBN: 978-0-06-135195-2
ISBN-10: 0-06-135195-4

07 08 09 10 11 OFF/UK 10 9 8 7 6 5 4 3 2 1

Contents

Introduction

Jane Austen and Charles Dickens belonged to different worlds. Austen was born into solid middle-class respectability in 1775. Her father, George, was an Oxford-educated clergyman and her mother, Cassandra (née Leigh), the daughter of another. She grew up living a comfortable, bucolic existence in her father's Hampshire rectory. Born in 1812, Charles Dickens also experienced an early childhood in the county of Hampshire. But his youthful idyll came to an end in 1824 when his father was thrown into gaol for debt and he found himself an apprentice in a boot-blacking factory near the Strand in London. Dickens never overcame the sense of degradation he felt after this rapid decline in social status.

Such differences in personal history go a long way towards explaining both the relative narrowness of Austen's literary canvas – a predilection for the marital and moral dilemmas of the rural well-to-do – and Dickens' ability to write about virtually the entire gamut of English society: from gentlefolk and factory owners to poor seamstresses and metropolitan pickpockets. Yet there are also similarities between them. Both are rightly esteemed as brilliant practitioners of their craft, and both dramatised human foibles with often withering satire. Moreover, Austen and Dickens did something highly unusual for either the budding or the established novelist: they wrote histories of their native land. Austen's rambunctious *The History of England from the Reign of Henry the 4th to the Death of Charles the 1st* and an excerpt from Dickens' more serious *A Child's History of England* are here presented together as powerful demonstrations of the way in which life experiences shape not only works of fiction but also attitudes to the past. Individually, they are also under-appreciated gems of English literature.

Austen produced her *History of England* in 1791 at the age of sixteen. It comprises just 34 pages of manuscript supported by thirteen watercolour miniatures of English monarchs painted by her older sister, Cassandra. Charles Dickens wrote his *Child's History of England* in the early 1850s when already a hugely successful novelist with an international following. His was a far more substantial work, comprising 38 detailed chapters. The first deals with 'Ancient England and the Romans' and the last gives a highly compressed account of the 18th and 19th centuries. *A Child's History* was to appear on the curricula of British schoolchildren well into the 20th century; many thousands of young boys and girls first learned of Hereward the Wake, Wat Tyler, John Hampden and Oliver Cromwell from Dickens' fast-paced excursion through England's past.

In contrast, Jane Austen's *History of England* remained unpublished until 1922. This is not surprising, for Austen's history had been written for performance at home rather than publication. Although generally shy in public, as an adolescent Jane Austen entertained her family circle in the parlour of her father's rectory by reading novels out loud and, with the help of siblings and a cousin, recreating London stage successes. She also presented her own short satirical compositions. Her *History of England* is one of 29 unmistakably precocious works of juvenilia written for domestic amusement. These were preserved in three slim quarto notebooks now held by the British Library in London. Comprising short stories, brief epistolary novels and fictional letters, most of these early works are social comedies. All reveal a young woman who read voraciously but with a keen and often merciless cynicism. Austen's natural impulse was towards parody, and the sentimental excesses of romantic fiction offered her especially rich pickings. Thus in her short novel *Lesley Castle*, Austen mocked the affected generosity of young women's correspondence, as when her lead character unblushingly comments to her friend: 'How often have I wished that I possessed as little personal beauty as you do; that my figure was as inelegant; my face as unlovely; and my appearance as unpleasing as yours!' Elsewhere the story slips into the burlesque, with absurdly named characters like 'Lady Kickabout'.

Austen compiled her juvenilia at a time when James Gillray and Thomas Rowlandson had achieved fame for their savage caricatures of venal statesmen, physicians and lawyers. Yet few young women of her class, education and literary ability would have seen cutting satire as their *métier*. Her early writings reveal that, even as an adolescent, she had the moral detachment that allowed her to perceive in the social rituals of her day so much self-serving cant and egotism. By the time she completed the earliest version of *Pride and Prejudice* in August 1797, she had acquired a more restrained and measured voice; but the 'splinter of ice in the heart' that Graham Greene believed essential for the writer had made itself felt much earlier.

Austen's *History of England* is of a piece with her early fictional works. It too is a work of deliberate and often witty parody. Each crowned head in turn is subjected to the mocking satire of a self-confessed 'partial, prejudiced, & ignorant Historian'. Austen begins with Henry IV, who ascended to the throne 'after having prevailed on his cousin & predecessor Richard the 2d to resign it to him, & to retire for the rest of his Life to Pomfret Castle, where he happened to be murdered'. And she continues in the same vein of comic *naïveté*. Henry VI is excoriated for no other reason than his being a Lancastrian; Richard III is described as 'very respectable' on the grounds of belonging to the house of York; Henry VII was 'as great a villain as ever lived'; and Henry VIII's sole virtue was his 'not being *quite* so bad as his daughter Elizabeth', herself a 'pest to Society' who persecuted the most 'amiable' Mary Queen of Scots. These sketches are playful and amusing, but there is also the underlying cold-bloodedness that gives the novels of Austen's maturity their steel – she blithely remarks that 'Lord Cobham was burnt alive, but I forget what for'.

Such superficialities were for Austen a stylistic choice. Throughout her *History of England* Austen feigns ignorance, warning the reader at the start: 'N.B. There will be very few Dates in this History.' She goes on to talk of Henry VIII's 'amiable' wife 'Anna Bullen' and to excuse the brevity of her account of this king's reign on the grounds that 'It would be an affront to my Readers were I to suppose that they were not as well acquainted with the particulars of this King's reign as I am myself'. In a way that recalls Sellar and Yeatman's classic *1066 And All That*, Austen delights in getting the facts twisted, muddled or plain wrong. Indeed, the parallels between these two parodies are often very close. Sellar and Yeatman had similar fun with the inability of most people to remember correctly the names of Henry's six wives: 'Henry VIII [had] … VIII wives, memorable amongst whom are Katherine the Arrogant, Anne of Cloves, Lady Jane Austin and Anne Hathaway.' Perhaps Sellar and Yeatman drew inspiration from Austen's *History* and thus paid homage to their precursor.

And like the authors of *1066 And All That*, Austen's opinionated frivolousness had a point. More than whimsy, her *History of England* is a satire on the style of history writing and pedagogy to which young girls of her class and station were routinely subjected. Austen's implicit objection was to the vapidity of history education. Names, dates and events were usually learned by rote, a passionless instruction in dry facts that were later garbled and misconstrued. In the final paragraph, Austen admits that 'the recital of any Events (except what I make myself) is uninteresting to me'. And she exults in illustrating how little the bored student gained from lessons in English history. The few facts recalled were trivial or, like Cobham's death or the Earl of Essex putting his hand on his sword before Elizabeth I, rendered meaningless because all sense of historical context had been forgotten.

It is not surprising that conventional histories should have repelled a young woman with the raging imagination and wit of Jane Austen. In the minds of many of her contemporaries, historical writing was meant to be sober and instructive rather than entertaining or truth-seeking. Above all, history was felt to be a necessary diversion from other forms of literature. Generations of moralists expressed the view that history was especially suited to the female intellect; Lady Mary Wray explained in 1778 that histories proved most 'useful' because they inculcated 'illustrious patterns of virtue'. No less importantly, they offered young women a 'means of diverting their relish from the frivolous fictions of romances'. The tight-laced evangelical Hannah More, dubbed 'a bishop in petticoats' by the radical William Cobbett, considered history to be most useful in imparting religious values and undoing the 'mischief' of popular romances. Novels poured from the printing presses in the late 18th century, and public moralists fretted about the danger posed to a young girl's morals by the indelicacies of Henry Fielding or Laurence Sterne. History, in contrast, kept the passions in check. But for Jane Austen, the staid histories written for popular consumption were intellectually insipid. They typified the schooling of young women, which she would attack in several of her novels for providing young ladies with 'Accomplishments' but leaving their 'Understanding unimproved ... and a Mind totally devoid of Taste and Judgment'.

The *History of England* also gives notice of Austen's antagonism towards sentimental excess and the 18th-century 'cult of sensibility'. She declares uncritical support for the House of York as a means of mocking the gratuitous partisanship of historical biographies; Charles I, for instance, is exonerated of all crimes against his people because of his Stuart blood. And her assertion that Anna Bullen's (*sic*) 'Beauty, her Elegance, & her Sprightliness were sufficient proofs' against charges of adultery lampoons the sentimentality of so many historical (and personal) judgements. Austen exaggerates the style of popular histories by packing her own full of their romantic clichés. Her special pleading on behalf of Mary Queen of Scots is especially well done. Mary's misfortunes are said to have arisen from nothing more than 'Imprudencies into which she was betrayed by the openness of her Heart, her Youth, & her Education'. A champion of sound common sense, Austen felt this kind of uncritical hyperbole deserved the severest satire.

In later years, Austen's views on official history became yet harder. In her send-up of the Gothic novel, *Northanger Abbey* (1798), the character Catherine Morland declares that she reads history 'a little as a duty, but it tells me nothing that does not either vex or weary me. The quarrels of popes and kings, with wars or pestilences, in every page.' Catherine goes so far as to say that history writing is no truer than fiction, and a good deal less engaging. Reminiscent of the feminism of Mary Wollstonecraft, Austen also has Catherine complain that in history, as typically written, 'the men are all so good for nothing, and [there are] hardly any women at all'. The same objection reappears in her last novel, *Persuasion* (1814), in which Anne Elliot declares herself to be well aware of the marginalisation of women in standard histories. Hence, in debating the constancy of women with Captain Harville, she asserts: 'Men have had every advantage to us in telling their own story. Education has been theirs in so much higher a degree; the pen has been in their hands. I will not allow books to prove anything.' Although there are no hints of feminism in *The History of England*, Austen already understood that most writers of history were hardly less prejudiced than the Yorkist narrator of her own spoof. In writing it, she took her revenge on both the tedium of contemporary pedagogy and the contrived sentimentality of scores of popular romances and histories.

To appreciate fully Austen's *History of England* it is necessary to recognise the targets of its satire, for this is anything but inconsequential juvenilia. While it cannot be classed as brilliant prose, *The History of England* is often sharply amusing and there are repeated hints of the penetrating irony of the mature author of *Pride and Prejudice.* It is the work of an exceptionally bright, if jaundiced, teenager imbued with the egoism and flippancy to be expected of such provenance. As she matured, Austen's characterisations became more subtle, though no less satirical. In fact, perhaps the most valuable thing about her history is the glimpse it gives us of a highly talented adolescent on her way to greatness.

When Charles Dickens completed his *Child's History of England* in 1853 he had already established a reputation as one of the finest novelists of his day. Ostensibly written for his children, and dictated to his wife's sister, Georgina Hogarth, his history was first published in instalments in his own journal, *Household Words*, between January 1851 and December 1853. Although far from conventional, *A Child's History* was quite unlike Austen's comic version of England's past. Dickens wrote a much more familiar chronological catalogue of monarchs, battles, beheadings, plagues, invasions and plots, with the expected complement of good and bad kings, wise and evil ministers, and assorted heroes and villains. In the excerpt included here, he takes the reader on a rollicking journey from the coronation of Elizabeth I through the travails of Mary Queen of Scots, the defeat of the Spanish Armada, the follies of James I and the sidelining of the Stuart Parliament, to Civil War and regicide. In many ways, Dickens plots a predictable course, using the same bearings to be found in the standard histories of England available to him. Indeed, in writing it he drew extensively on Thomas Keightley's *History of England* and Charles Knight's *Pictorial History of England* (his copy of the latter is heavily marked). The result was the kind of date-abundant, male-centred history against which Jane Austen had rebelled half a century earlier. Had she lived long enough to do so, Austen might well have had fun satirising *A Child's History*, in which even the names of the main characters are capitalised.

Even so, she would have seen plenty to admire in this work. Here and there in *A Child's History* we see Dickens near the height of his powers: combining a mastery of plain language, sharp if sometimes heavy irony, and the keenest eye for evocative detail. Some passages, such as the description of the execution of Mary Queen of Scots, are particularly arresting. Dickens tells of how, as Mary's severed head was lifted above the executioner's block, her red wig fell off, revealing hair 'as grey as that of a woman of seventy'. But while all 'her beauty was gone', Dickens wrote, she 'was beautiful enough to her little dog, who cowered under her dress, frightened, when she went on the scaffold, and who lay down beside her headless body when all her earthly sorrows were over'.

Austen also would have appreciated Dickens' humanity and sardonic wit. Throughout the book he shows himself wholly intolerant of the follies and arrogance of many of England's rulers, at whose feet he lays much of the blame for the copious 'turmoil and bloodshed' of his nation's history.

Henry VIII is deemed 'a blot of blood and grease' and 'one of the most detestable villains that ever drew breath', Elizabeth I is 'crafty', dishonest and over-rated, Mary Queen of Scots is a dangerous hothead, and James I is scandalously renamed 'his Sowship' and subjected to an indictment of several pages. In a letter to a friend, Dickens explained that he wanted his history to be more 'true' than 'genteel'. His natural sympathy lay with the 'people', not their rulers, a stance which was considered indecorous by many of his less politically radical contemporaries. While modern historians would question the veracity of his account, Dickens had no interest in serving up the bland fare that others may have felt more suitable for a child's palate – and less threatening to the status quo. His is sectarian history: radical, opinionated, and, to most readers, all the better for it.

Not all historians were so unforgiving of England's bloodier rulers. Dickens' contemporary, the Oxford University historian James Anthony Froude, considered Henry VIII's vandalism of monastic property excusable because the Reformation was 'the root and source of the expansive force which has spread the Anglo-Saxon race over the globe'. Dickens saw that this was mere special pleading. In contemplating Henry VIII he saw only a brutal tyrant to whose petty vanity were sacrificed the lives of thousands of innocent men and women, and whose henchmen, in dissolving the monasteries, destroyed some of the greatest works of medieval art and denied innumerable poor men and women their main source of help in an otherwise uncaring world. Generations of children had been taught to relish the marital and military antics of 'Bluff King Hal' and to view the demise of the monasteries as an essential step in freeing England from the malign authority of the Pope. Dickens considered this self-serving nonsense. He was interested in rights and wrongs, not long-term historical consequences. Sitting in stern judgement, he made virtually no allowance for differences in culture and outlook from one period to another. Dickens measured past leaders and rebels against his own moral and political sensibilities, and anybody found wanting was held to account.

This kind of approach is roundly rejected by modern historians, who emphasise the importance of historical context in judging past actions and the changeability of moral values over time. But it is easy enough to explain why Dickens' personal sympathies were largely reserved for the middle and the lower orders. Having experienced poverty, he was always ready to extend compassion to the underclasses. He did not look with haughty contempt upon those who were low-born and yet failed to rise as he had himself. The shame of having been poor served almost as a muse. With Dickens, therefore, there is no reflex deference to kings, lords and bishops. For him, the long history of brutality towards labouring men and women could not be a subject for flippancy or mirth, as it had been for the comfortably well-off Jane Austen. Nor did he want to blunt his history with more than a sprinkling of comedy. Rulers are awarded ticks by Dickens largely according to how many of their citizens' lives they restrained themselves from ending in petty feuds and dynastic rivalries. Few monarchs measure up well to this yardstick. Despite the affecting account he gives of her death, Mary Queen of Scots scores as badly as most. '[She] came to England', he writes, 'to her own ruin, the trouble of the kingdom, and the misery and death of many.' Sometimes his anti-patrician feelings come out more plainly, as when he remarks that the 'Court was not quite so honest as the people – but perhaps it sometimes is not'. And while falling short of actually condoning the execution of Charles I, Dickens reminds his young readers that he was no martyr who had first martyred his own people and ridden roughshod over their traditional liberties. Dickens doubtless concurred with the words he quotes as having been uttered by the Earl of Strafford, abandoned by Charles I to public execution: 'Put not your trust in Princes!'

From reading *A Child's History*, no less than *Hard Times*, we can see why his first biographer, John Forster, asserted that Dickens 'secretly resented … inequalities of rank'. Similarly, one can understand why the poet, politician and historian, Thomas Babington Macaulay, accused him of 'sullen socialism'. In reality, however, Dickens was never a fire-breathing radical. While he accepted that growing up amid the rookeries of London's slums might tend to corrupt a child's character, he remained a moral individualist. Wholly in keeping with mid-Victorian attitudes towards the lower classes, his fictional creations were seen to have moral choices, and when they sank they did so because they chose vice over virtue. Nancy in *Oliver Twist* illustrates Dickens' implicit belief that redemption was possible even for the wicked, and that those – like Fagin and Sikes – who did not avail themselves of the opportunity deserved their grisly fates. Hence there is hardly a hint in *A Child's History* of a sociological analysis. Dickens clearly sees the demise of feudalism and the strengthening of parliament as embodying real historical progress. But everyone from rulers and generals to magistrates and yeomen are judged as individuals rather than as the products of their particular cultures or circumstances. Dickens' novels, short stories and journalism provided evidence that inspired plenty of others to mount critiques of inequality and the class system, but he seldom did so himself. For all his seeming radicalism, he remained a spokesman for the Victorian middle class.

Beneath Dickens' historical judgements lay the common bourgeois presumption that the wicked eventually got their comeuppance. A prisoner of Victorian moral sensibilities, he could not face up to the paradox noted by Sir Winston Churchill in his own history of England that 'capable rulers by their very virtues sow the seeds of future evil, and weak or degenerate princes open the pathway to progress'. Dickens' approach to writing history lacked both intellectual sophistication and cultural detachment. But to think in radically new ways about the past had never been his aim. For Dickens, history provided material to criticise the flaws and foibles and celebrate the virtues of a timeless range of human character types. Nor was he alone in this approach. As J.A. Froude put it: 'One lesson, and only one, history may be said to repeat with distinctness; that the world is built somehow on moral foundations; that, in the long run, it is well with the good; in the long run it is ill with the wicked.' To which, one suspects, the more knowing Miss Austen would have replied: 'But that it were so!'

Dickens also shared Froude's belief that the achievements of the English peoples in the previous decades showed that right ultimately did prevail. Like most of his generation, Dickens felt a deep pride in his nation's record of economic and imperial expansion. The period's soaring spirit of optimism infused his *Child's History*, the writing of which coincided with the opening of that spectacular celebration of English superiority in almost all things new, the Great Exhibition of 1851. According to Dickens, the achievements that this event extolled were the realisation of the superiority of the 'English-Saxon', which itself represented 'the greatest character among the nations of the earth'. This sense of racial destiny conformed closely to the prevailing stereotypes of his day. Elsewhere he expresses the view that, wherever the 'English-Saxon' race went, 'there, law and industry, and safety for life and property, and all the great results of perseverance, are certain to arise'.

Self-congratulatory and ethnocentric though these attitudes were, there is no might-equals-right jingoism in *A Child's History*. Dickens wrote about race and nationality as most Britons did at a time when British manufactures were advancing so rapidly that all but the most self-deprecating were bound to see themselves as specially endowed or favoured by God. The idea that the major currents of human history could be reduced to the conflicts among intellectually unequal races was becoming virtually a staple of ethnological thought during the 1850s. Unlike many, however, Dickens saw the excellence of his race not so much in imperial expansion or the opening of new markets to English wares as in the spread of moral enlightenment and the rule of law. Even here we find abundant evidence of Dickens' humanity.

A Child's History was long favoured by the British educational establishment. Successive editions were published from the 1850s through to the Second World War. Thereafter its appeal faded. To some extent this was due to the spread of the more exacting standards of historical scholarship and interpretation that had been introduced by German scholars during the 1800s. Their approach placed emphasis on context and the use of abundant original sources. But the precipitous decline in the book's popularity from the 1950s suggests that deeper trends may have been at work. The credibility of the optimistic histories written in the mid-Victorian age, like *A Child's History*, was surely undercut by the experience of a second major European blood-letting and the gradual relegation of Britain from imperial superpower to also-ran. By the 1950s, fewer and fewer Britons saw the present as a triumphant culmination of the past. *A Child's History* had begun to look badly dated.

So what is its value to posterity? For the Catholic theologian, novelist and critic, G.K. Chesterton, writing in 1911, the chief worth of *A Child's History* lay in its holding a mirror up to the mid-Victorian age. 'The history tells us', Chesterton explained, 'nothing about the periods that it talks about; but it tells us a great deal about the period that it does not talk about; the period in which it was written.' This is a harsh judgement and an obvious overstatement; but it contains a large kernel of truth. The world Dickens knew largely set the agenda for what he included in his history and how he interpreted it. This is of course true for all histories, even the most modern or abstruse. But Dickens' exceptional gift for articulating the feelings and concerns of the middle class means that the content and tone of his history conveys a reliable sense of the attitudes of a large part of Victorian society. It was because Dickens shared his sense of what was important with much of his vast readership that the ever-perceptive novelist Anthony Trollope dubbed him 'Mr Popular Sentiment'. Read as a historical source, *A Child's History* gives rich insights into a culture that had a very different relationship with the past (real and imagined) than Britons do a century and a half later. It is, incidentally, ironic that, in spite of his political radicalism, Dickens wrote a more conformist history than the rather more genteel Jane Austen.

Yet *A Child's History* and Austen's *History of England* are not merely valuable historical relics. They both deserve to be read not just because of what they tell us about the authors and their times, but because they are written with a freshness and wit of which only great writers are capable.

David Starkey
July 2006

The History of England
from the reign of
Henry the 4th
to the death of
Charles the 1st

By a partial, prejudiced, & ignorant Historian.

To Miss Austen eldest daughter of the Revd George Austen, this book is inscribed with all due respect by
The Author

N.B. There will be very few Dates in this History.

Henry the 4th

Henry the 4th ascended the throne of England much to his own satisfaction in the year 1399, after having prevailed on his cousin & predecessor Richard the 2d to resign it to him, & to retire for the rest of his Life to Pomfret Castle, where he happened to be murdered. It is to be supposed that Henry was married, since he had certainly four sons, but it is not in my power to inform the Reader who was his wife. Be this as it may, he did not live for ever, but falling ill, his son the Prince of Wales came and took away the crown; whereupon, the King made a long speech, for which I must refer the Reader to Shakespear's Plays, & the Prince made a still longer. Things being thus settled between them the King died, & was succeeded by his son Henry who had previously beat Sir William Gascoigne.

Henry the 5th

This Prince after he succeeded to the throne grew quite reformed & amiable, forsaking all his dissipated Companions, & never thrashing Sir William again. During his reign, Lord Cobham was burnt alive, but I forget what for. His Majesty then turned his thoughts to France, where he went & fought the famous Battle of Agincourt. He afterwards married the King's daughter Catherine, a very agreable Woman by Shakespear's account. Inspite of all this however he died, and was succeeded by his son Henry.

Henry the 6th

I cannot say much for this Monarch's Sense. Nor would I if I could, for he was a Lancastrian. I suppose you know all about the Wars between him & the Duke of York who was of the right side; if you do not, you had better read some other History, for I shall not be very diffuse in this, meaning by it only to vent my Spleen *against*, & shew my Hatred *to* all those people whose parties or principles do not suit with mine, & not to give information. This King married Margaret of Anjou, a woman whose distresses & Misfortunes were so great as almost to make me who hate her, pity her. It was in this reign that Joan of Arc lived & made such a *row* among the English. They should not have burnt her—but they did. There were several Battles between the Yorkists & Lancastrians, in which the former (as they ought) usually conquered. At length they were entirely overcome; The King was murdered—The Queen was sent home—& Edward the 4th ascended the Throne.

Edward the 4th

This Monarch was famous only for his Beauty & his Courage, of which the Picture we have here given of him, & his undaunted Behaviour in marrying one Woman while he was engaged to another, are sufficient proofs. His Wife was Elizabeth Woodville, a Widow who, poor woman! was afterwards confined in a Convent by that Monster of Iniquity & Avarice Henry the 7th. One of Edward's Mistresses was Jane Shore, who has had a play written about her, but it is a tragedy & therefore not worth reading. Having performed all these noble actions, his Majesty died, & was succeeded by his son.

Edward the 5th

This unfortunate Prince lived so little a while that nobody had time to draw his picture. He was murdered by his Uncle's Contrivance, whose name was Richard the 3d.

Richard the 3d

The Character of this Prince has been in general very severely treated by Historians, but as he was a *York*, I am rather inclined to suppose him a very respectable Man. It has indeed been confidently asserted that he killed his two Nephews & his Wife, but it has also been declared that he did *not* kill his two Nephews, which I am inclined to beleive true; & if this is the case, it may also be affirmed that he did not kill his Wife, for if Perkin Warbeck was really the Duke of York, why might not Lambert Simnel be the Widow of Richard. Whether innocent or guilty, he did not reign long in peace, for Henry Tudor Earl of Richmond as great a Villain as ever lived, made a great fuss about getting the Crown & having killed the King at the battle of Bosworth, he succeeded to it.

Henry the 7th

This Monarch soon after his accession married the Princess Elizabeth of York, by which alliance he plainly proved that he thought his own right inferior to hers, tho' he pretended to the contrary. By this marriage he had two sons & two daughters, the elder of which Daughters was married to the King of Scotland & had the happiness of being grandmother to one of the first Characters in the World. But of *her*, I shall have occasion to speak more at large in future. The Youngest, Mary, married first the King of France & secondly the Duke of Suffolk, by whom she had one daughter, afterwards the Mother of Lady Jane Gray, who tho' inferior to her lovely Cousin the Queen of Scots, was yet an amiable young woman & famous for reading Greek while other people were hunting. It was in the reign of Henry the 7th that Perkin Warbeck & Lambert Simnel before mentioned made their appearance, the former of whom was set in the Stocks, took shelter in Beaulieu Abbey, & was beheaded with the Earl of Warwick, & the latter was taken into the Kings kitchen. His Majesty died & was succeeded by his son Henry whose only merit was his not being *quite* so bad as his daughter Elizabeth.

Henry the 8th

It would be an affront to my Readers were I to suppose that they were not as well acquainted with the particulars of this King's reign as I am myself.

It will therefore be saving *them* the task of reading again what they have read before, & *myself* the trouble of writing what I do not perfectly recollect, by giving only a slight sketch of the principal Events which marked his reign. Among these may be ranked Cardinal Wolsey's telling the father Abbott of Leicester Abbey that 'he was come to lay his bones among them,' the reformation in Religion, & the King's riding through the streets of London with Anna Bullen. It is however but Justice, & my Duty to declare that this amiable Woman was entirely innocent of the Crimes with which she was accused, of which her Beauty, her Elegance, & her Sprightliness were sufficient proofs, not to mention her solemn protestations of Innocence, the weakness of the Charges against her, & the King's Character, all of which add some confirmation, tho' perhaps but slight ones when in comparison with those before alledged in her favour. Tho' I do not profess giving many dates, yet as I think it proper to give some & shall of course make choice of those which it is most necessary for the Reader to know, I think it right to inform him that her letter to the King was dated on the 6th of May. The Crimes & Cruelties of this Prince, were too numerous to be mentioned, (as this history I trust has fully shewn;) & nothing can be said in his vindication, but that his abolishing Religious Houses & leaving them to the ruinous depredations of time has been of infinite use to the landscape of England in general, which probably was a principal motive for his doing it, since otherwise why should a Man who was of no Religion himself be at so much trouble to abolish one which had for Ages been established in the Kingdom. His Majesty's 5th wife was the Duke of Norfolk's Neice who, tho' universally acquitted of the crimes for which she was beheaded, has been by many people supposed to have led an abandoned life before her Marriage—Of this however I have many doubts, since she was a relation of that noble Duke of Norfolk who was so warm in the Queen of Scotland's cause, & who at last fell a victim to it. The King's last wife contrived to survive him, but with difficulty effected it. He was succeeded by his only son Edward.

Edward the 6th

As this prince was only nine years old at the time of his Father's death, he was considered by many people as too young to govern, & the late King happening to be of the same opinion, his mother's Brother the Duke of Somerset was chosen Protector of the realm during his minority. This Man was on the whole of a very amiable Character, & is somewhat of a favourite with me, tho' I would by no means pretend to affirm that he was equal to those first of Men Robert Earl of Essex, Delamere, or Gilpin. He was beheaded, of which he might with reason have been proud, had he known that such was the death of Mary Queen of Scotland; but as it was impossible that he should be conscious of what had never happened, it does not appear that he felt particularly delighted with the manner of it. After his decease the Duke of Northumberland had the care of the King & the Kingdom, & performed his trust of both so well that the King died & the Kingdom was left to his daughter in law the Lady Jane Grey, who has been already mentioned as reading Greek. Whether she really understood that language or whether such a study proceeded only from an excess of vanity for which I beleive she was always rather remarkable, is uncertain. Whatever might be the cause, she preserved the same appearance of knowledge, & contempt of what was generally esteemed pleasure, during the whole of her Life, for she declared herself displeased with being appointed Queen, and while conducting to the Scaffold, she wrote a sentence in Latin & another in Greek on seeing the dead Body of her Husband accidentally passing that way.

Mary

This Woman had the good luck of being advanced to the throne of England, inspite of the superior pretensions, Merit & Beauty of her Cousins Mary Queen of Scotland & Jane Grey. Nor can I pity the Kingdom for the misfortunes they experienced during her Reign, since they fully deserved them, for having allowed her to succeed her Brother—which was a double peice of folly, since they might have foreseen that as she died without Children, she would be succeeded by that disgrace to humanity, that pest of society, Elizabeth. Many were the people who fell Martyrs to the protestant Religion during her reign; I suppose not fewer than a dozen. She married Philip King of Spain who in her Sister's reign for [*sic*] famous for building the Armadas. She died without issue, & then the dreadful moment came in which the destroyer of all comfort, the deceitful Betrayer of trust reposed in her, & the Murderess of her Cousin succeeded to the Throne.—

Elizabeth

It was the peculiar misfortune of this Woman to have bad Ministers—Since wicked as she herself was, she could not have committed such extensive Mischeif, had not those vile & abandoned Men connived at, & encouraged her in her Crimes. I know that it has by many people been asserted & beleived that Lord Burleigh, Sir Francis Walsingham, & the rest of those who filled the cheif Offices of State were deserving, experienced, & able Ministers. But oh! how blinded such Writers & such Readers must be to true Merit, to Merit despised, neglected & defamed, if they can persist in such opinions when they reflect that these Men, these boasted Men were such Scandals to their Country & their Sex as to allow & assist their Queen in confining for the space of nineteen Years, a *Woman* who if the claims of Relationship & Merit were of no avail, yet as a Queen & as one who condescended to place confidence in her, had every reason to expect Assistance & protection; and at length in allowing Elizabeth to bring this amiable Woman to an untimely, unmerited, and scandalous Death. Can any one if he reflects but for a moment on this blot, this ever-lasting blot upon their Understanding & their Character, allow any praise to Lord Burleigh or Sir Francis Walsingham? Oh! what must this bewitching Princess whose only freind was then the Duke of Norfolk, and whose only ones are now Mr Whitaker, Mrs Lefroy, Mrs Knight & myself, who was abandoned by her Son, confined by her Cousin, abused, reproached & vilified by all, what must not her most noble mind have suffered when informed that Elizabeth had given orders for her Death! Yet she bore it with a most unshaken fortitude, firm in her Mind; Constant in her Religion; & prepared herself to meet the cruel fate to which she was doomed, with a magnanimity that could alone proceed from conscious Innocence. And yet could you Reader have beleived it possible that some hardened & zealous Protestants have even abused her for that Steadfastness in the Catholic Religion which reflected on her so much credit? But this is a striking proof of *their* narrow souls & prejudiced

Judgements who accuse her. She was executed in the Great Hall at Fotheringay Castle (sacred Place!) on Wednesday the 8th of February—1586—to the everlasting Reproach of Elizabeth, her Ministers, and of England in general. It may not be unnecessary before I entirely conclude my account of this ill-fated Queen, to observe that she had been accused of several crimes during the time of her reigning in Scotland, of which I now most seriously do assure my Reader that she was entirely innocent; having never been guilty of anything more than Imprudencies into which she was betrayed by the openness of her Heart, her Youth, & her Education. Having I trust by this assurance entirely done away every Suspicion & every doubt which might have arisen in the Reader's mind, from what other Historians have written of her, I shall proceed to mention the remaining Events that marked Elizabeth's reign. It was about this time that Sir Francis Drake the first English Navigator who sailed round the World, lived, to be the ornament of his Country & his profession. Yet great as he was, & justly celebrated as a Sailor, I cannot help foreseeing that he will be equalled in this or the next Century by one who tho' now but young, already promises to answer all the ardent & sanguine expectations of his Relations & Freinds, amongst whom I may class the amiable Lady to whom this work is dedicated, & my no less amiable Self.

Though of a different profession, and shining in a different Sphere of Life, yet equally conspicuous in the Character of an *Earl*, as Drake was in that of a *Sailor*, was Robert Devereux Lord Essex. This unfortunate young Man was not unlike in Character to that equally unfortunate one *Frederic Delamere*. The simile may be carried still farther, & Elizabeth the torment of Essex may be compared to the Emmeline of Delamere. It would be endless to recount the misfortunes of this noble & gallant Earl. It is sufficient to say that he was beheaded on the 25th of February, after having been Lord Leuitenant of Ireland, after having clapped his hand on his Sword, and after performing many other services to his Country. Elizabeth did not long survive his loss, & died *so* miserable that were it not an injury to the memory of Mary I should pity her.

James the 1st

Though this King had some faults, among which & as the most principal, was his allowing his

Mother's death, yet considered on the whole I cannot help liking him. He married Anne of Denmark, and had several Children; fortunately for him his eldest son Prince Henry died before his Father or he might have experienced the evils which befell his unfortunate Brother.

As I am myself partial to the roman catholic religion, it is with infinite regret that I am obliged to blame the Behaviour of any Member of it; yet Truth being I think very excusable in an Historian, I am necessitated to say that in this reign the roman Catholics of England did not behave like Gentlemen to the protestants. Their Behaviour indeed to the Royal Family & both Houses of Parliament might justly be considered by them as very uncivil, and even Sir Henry Percy tho' certainly the best bred man of the party, had none of that general politeness which is so universally pleasing, as his attentions were entirely confined to Lord Mounteagle.

Sir Walter Raleigh flourished in this & the preceding reign, & is by many people held in great veneration & respect—But as he was an enemy of the noble Essex, I have nothing to say in praise of him, & must refer all those who may wish to be acquainted with the particulars of his Life, to Mr Sheridan's play of the Critic, where they will find many interesting Anecdotes as well of him as of his freind Sir Christopher Hatton.—His Majesty was of that amiable disposition which inclines to Freindship, & in such points was possessed of a keener penetration in Discovering Merit than many other people. I once heard an excellent sharade on a Carpet, of which the subject I am now on reminds me, and as I think it may afford my Readers some amusement to *find it out*, I shall here take the liberty of presenting it to them.

Sharade
My first is what my second was to King James the 1st, and you tread on my whole.

The principal favourites of his Majesty were Car, who was afterwards created Earl of Somerset and whose name perhaps may have some share in the above-mentioned Sharade, & George Villiers afterwards Duke of Buckingham. On his Majesty's death he was succeeded by his son Charles.

Charles the 1st

This amiable Monarch seems born to have suffered Misfortunes equal to those of his lovely Grandmother; Misfortunes which he could not deserve since he was her descendant. Never certainly were there before so many detestable Characters at one time in England as in this period of its History; Never were amiable Men so scarce. The number of them throughout the whole Kingdom amounting only to *five*, besides the inhabitants of Oxford who were always loyal to their King & faithful to his interests. The names of this noble five who never forgot the duty of the Subject, or swerved from their attachment to his Majesty, were as follows—The King himself, ever steadfast in his own support—Archbishop Laud, Earl of Strafford, Viscount Faulkland, & Duke of Ormond, who were scarcely less strenuous or zealous in the cause. While the *Villains* of the time would make too long a list to be written or read; I shall therefore content myself with mentioning the leaders of the Gang. Cromwell, Fairfax, Hampden, & Pym may be considered as the original Causers of all the disturbances, Distresses, & Civil Wars in which England for many years was embroiled. In this reign as well as in that of Elizabeth, I am obliged in spite of my attachment to the Scotch, to consider them as equally guilty with the generality of the English, since they dared to think differently from their Sovereign, to forget the Adoration which as *Stuarts* it was their Duty to pay them, to rebel against, dethrone & imprison the unfortunate Mary; to oppose, to deceive, and to sell the no less unfortunate Charles. The Events of this Monarch's reign are too numerous for my pen, and indeed the recital of any Events (except what I make myself) is uninteresting to me; my principal reason for undertaking the History of England being to prove the innocence of the Queen of Scotland, which I flatter myself with having effectually done, and to abuse Elizabeth, tho' I am rather fearful of having fallen short in the latter part of my Scheme. –As therefore it is not my intention to give any particular account of the distresses into which this King was involved through the misconduct & Cruelty of his Parliament, I shall satisfy myself with vindicating him from the Reproach of arbitrary & tyrannical Government with which he has often been charged. This, I feel, is not difficult to be done, for with one argument I am certain of satisfying every sensible & well disposed person whose opinions have been properly guided by a good Education—& this Argument is that he was a Stuart.

Finis

Saturday Nov: 26th. 1791

Excerpt from

A Child's History of England

by Charles Dickens

England under Elizabeth

There was great rejoicing all over the land when the Lords of the Council went down to Hatfield, to hail the Princess Elizabeth as the new Queen of England. Weary of the barbarities of Mary's reign, the people looked with hope and gladness to the new Sovereign. The nation seemed to wake from a horrible dream; and Heaven, so long hidden by the smoke of the fires that roasted men and women to death, appeared to brighten once more.

Queen Elizabeth was five-and-twenty years of age when she rode through the streets of London, from the Tower to Westminster Abbey, to be crowned. Her countenance was strongly marked, but on the whole, commanding and dignified; her hair was red, and her nose something too long and sharp for a woman's. She was not the beautiful creature her courtiers made out; but she was well enough, and no doubt looked all the better for coming after the dark and gloomy Mary. She was well educated, but a roundabout writer, and rather a hard swearer and coarse talker. She was clever, but cunning and deceitful, and inherited much of her father's violent temper. I mention this now, because she has been so over-praised by one party, and so over-abused by another, that it is hardly possible to understand the greater part of her reign without first understanding what kind of woman she really was.

She began her reign with the great advantage of having a very wise and careful Minister, SIR WILLIAM CECIL, whom she afterwards made LORD BURLEIGH. Altogether, the people had greater reason for rejoicing than they usually had, when there were processions in the streets; and they were happy with some reason. All kinds of shows and images were set up; GOG and MAGOG were hoisted to the top of Temple Bar, and (which was more to the purpose) the Corporation dutifully presented the young Queen with the sum of a thousand marks in gold—so heavy a present, that she was obliged to take it into her carriage with both hands. The coronation was a great success; and, on the next day, one of the courtiers presented a petition to the new Queen, praying that as it was the custom to release some prisoners on such occasions, she would have the goodness to release the four Evangelists, Matthew, Mark, Luke, and John, and also the Apostle Saint Paul, who had been for some time shut up in a strange language so that the people could not get at them.

To this, the Queen replied that it would be better first to inquire of themselves whether they desired to be released or not; and, as a means of finding out, a great public discussion—a sort of religious tournament—was appointed to take place between certain champions of the two religions, in Westminster Abbey. You may suppose that it was soon made pretty clear to common sense, that for people to benefit by what they repeat or read, it is rather necessary they should understand something about it. Accordingly, a Church Service in plain English was settled, and other laws and regulations were made, completely establishing the great work of the Reformation. The Romish bishops and champions were not harshly dealt with, all things considered; and the Queen's Ministers were both prudent and merciful.

The one great trouble of this reign, and the unfortunate cause of the greater part of such turmoil and bloodshed as occurred in it, was MARY STUART, QUEEN OF SCOTS. We will try to understand, in as few words as possible, who Mary was, what she was, and how she came to be a thorn in the royal pillow of Elizabeth. She was the daughter of the Queen Regent of Scotland, MARY OF GUISE. She had been married, when a mere child, to the Dauphin, the son and heir of the King of France. The Pope, who pretended that no one could rightfully wear the crown of England without his gracious permission, was strongly opposed to Elizabeth, who had not asked for the said gracious permission. And as Mary Queen of Scots would have inherited the English crown in right of her birth, supposing the English Parliament not to have altered the succession, the Pope himself, and most of the discontented who were followers of his, maintained that Mary was the rightful Queen of England, and Elizabeth the wrongful Queen. Mary being so closely connected with France, and France being jealous of England, there was far greater danger in this than there would have been if she had had no alliance with that great power. And when her young husband, on the death of his father, became FRANCIS THE SECOND, King of France, the matter grew very serious. For, the young couple styled themselves King and Queen of England, and the Pope was disposed to help them by doing all the mischief he could.

Now, the reformed religion, under the guidance of a stern and powerful preacher, named JOHN KNOX, and other such men, had been making fierce progress in Scotland. It was still a half savage country, where there was a great deal of murdering and rioting continually going on; and the Reformers, instead of reforming those evils as they should have done, went to work in the ferocious old Scottish spirit, laying churches and chapels waste, pulling down pictures and altars, and knocking about the Grey Friars, and the Black Friars, and the White Friars, and the friars of all sorts of colours, in all directions. This obdurate and harsh spirit of the Scottish Reformers (the Scotch have always been rather a sullen and frowning people in religious matters) put up the blood of the Romish French court, and caused France to send troops over to Scotland, with the hope of setting the friars of all sorts of colours on their legs again; of conquering that country first, and England afterwards; and so crushing the Reformation all to pieces. The Scottish Reformers, who had formed a great league which they called The Congregation of the Lord, secretly represented to Elizabeth that, if the reformed religion got the worst of it with them, it would be likely to get the worst of it in England too; and thus, Elizabeth, though she had a high notion of the rights of Kings and Queens to do anything they liked, sent an army to Scotland to support the Reformers, who were in arms against their sovereign. All these proceedings led to a treaty of peace at Edinburgh, under which the French consented to depart from the kingdom. By a separate treaty, Mary and her young husband engaged to renounce their assumed title of King and Queen of England. But this treaty they never fulfilled.

It happened, soon after matters had got to this state, that the young French King died, leaving Mary a young widow. She was then invited by her Scottish subjects to return home and reign over them; and as she was not now happy where she was, she, after a little time, complied.

Elizabeth had been Queen three years, when Mary Queen of Scots embarked at Calais for her own rough, quarrelling country. As she came out of the harbour, a vessel was lost before her eyes, and she said, 'O! good God! what an omen this is for such a voyage!' She was very fond of France, and sat on the deck, looking back at it and weeping, until it was quite dark. When she went to bed, she directed to be called at daybreak, if the French coast were still visible, that she might behold it for the last time. As it proved to be a clear morning, this was done, and she again wept for the country she was leaving, and said many times, 'Farewell, France! Farewell, France! I shall never see thee again!' All this was long remembered afterwards, as sorrowful and interesting in a fair young princess of nineteen. Indeed, I am afraid it gradually came, together with her other distresses, to surround her with greater sympathy than she deserved.

When she came to Scotland, and took up her abode at the palace of Holyrood in Edinburgh, she found herself among uncouth strangers and wild uncomfortable customs very different from her experiences in the court of France. The very people who were disposed to love her, made her head ache when she was tired out by her voyage, with a serenade of discordant music—a fearful concert of bagpipes, I suppose—and brought her and her train home to her palace on miserable little Scotch horses that appeared to be half starved. Among the people who were not disposed to love her, she found the powerful leaders of the Reformed

Church, who were bitter upon her amusements, however innocent, and denounced music and dancing as works of the devil. John Knox himself often lectured her, violently and angrily, and did much to make her life unhappy. All these reasons confirmed her old attachment to the Romish religion, and caused her, there is no doubt, most imprudently and dangerously both for herself and for England too, to give a solemn pledge to the heads of the Romish Church that if she ever succeeded to the English crown, she would set up that religion again. In reading her unhappy history, you must always remember this; and also that during her whole life she was constantly put forward against the Queen, in some form or other, by the Romish party.

That Elizabeth, on the other hand, was not inclined to like her, is pretty certain. Elizabeth was very vain and jealous, and had an extraordinary dislike to people being married. She treated Lady Catherine Grey, sister of the beheaded Lady Jane, with such shameful severity, for no other reason than her being secretly married, that she died and her husband was ruined; so, when a second marriage for Mary began to be talked about, probably Elizabeth disliked her more. Not that Elizabeth wanted suitors of her own, for they started up from Spain, Austria, Sweden, and England. Her English lover at this time, and one whom she much favoured too, was LORD ROBERT DUDLEY, Earl of Leicester—himself secretly married to AMY ROBSART, the daughter of an English gentleman, whom he was strongly suspected of causing to be murdered, down at his country seat, Cumnor Hall in Berkshire, that he might be free to marry the Queen. Upon this story, the great writer, SIR WALTER SCOTT, has founded one of his best romances. But if Elizabeth knew how to lead her handsome favourite on, for her own vanity and pleasure, she knew how to stop him for her own pride; and his love, and all the other proposals, came to nothing. The Queen always declared in good set speeches, that she would never be married at all, but would live and die a Maiden Queen. It was a very pleasant and meritorious declaration, I suppose; but it has been puffed and trumpeted so much, that I am rather tired of it myself.

Divers princes proposed to marry Mary, but the English court had reasons for being jealous of them all, and even proposed as a matter of policy that she should marry that very Earl of Leicester who had aspired to be the husband of Elizabeth. At last, LORD DARNLEY, son of the Earl of Lennox, and himself descended from the Royal Family of Scotland, went over with Elizabeth's consent to try his fortune at Holyrood. He was a tall simpleton; and could dance and play the guitar; but I know of nothing else he could do, unless it were to get very drunk, and eat gluttonously, and make a contemptible spectacle of himself in many mean and vain ways. However, he gained Mary's heart, not disdaining in the pursuit of his object to ally himself with one of her secretaries, DAVID RIZZIO, who had great influence with her. He soon married the Queen. This marriage does not say much for her, but what followed will presently say less.

Mary's brother, the EARL OF MURRAY, and head of the Protestant party in Scotland, had opposed this marriage, partly on religious grounds, and partly perhaps from personal dislike of the very contemptible bridegroom. When it had taken place through Mary's gaining over to it the more powerful of the lords about her, she banished

Murray for his pains; and, when he and some other nobles rose in arms to support the reformed religion, she herself, within a month of her wedding day, rode against them in armour with loaded pistols in her saddle. Driven out of Scotland, they presented themselves before Elizabeth—who called them traitors in public, and assisted them in private, according to her crafty nature.

Mary had been married but a little while, when she began to hate her husband, who, in his turn, began to hate that David Rizzio, with whom he had leagued to gain her favour, and whom he now believed to be her lover. He hated Rizzio to that extent, that he made a compact with LORD RUTHVEN and three other lords to get rid of him by murder. This wicked agreement they made in solemn secrecy upon the first of March, fifteen hundred and sixty-six, and on the night of Saturday the ninth, the conspirators were brought by Darnley up a private staircase, dark and steep, into a range of rooms where they knew that Mary was sitting at supper with her sister, Lady Argyle, and this doomed man. When they went into the room, Darnley took the Queen round the waist, and Lord Ruthven, who had risen from a bed of sickness to do this murder, came in, gaunt and ghastly, leaning on two men. Rizzio ran behind the Queen for shelter and protection. 'Let him come out of the room,' said Ruthven. 'He shall not leave the room,' replied the Queen; 'I read his danger in your face, and it is my will that he remain here.' They then set upon him, struggled with him, overturned the table, dragged him out, and killed him with fifty-six stabs. When the Queen heard that he was dead, she said, 'No more tears. I will think now of revenge!'

Within a day or two, she gained her husband over, and prevailed on the tall idiot to abandon the conspirators and fly with her to Dunbar. There, he issued a proclamation, audaciously and falsely denying that he had any knowledge of the late bloody business; and there they were joined by the EARL BOTHWELL and some other nobles. With their help, they raised eight thousand men; returned to Edinburgh, and drove the assassins into England. Mary soon afterwards gave birth to a son—still thinking of revenge.

That she should have had a greater scorn for her husband after his late cowardice and treachery than she had had before, was natural enough.

There is little doubt that she now began to love Bothwell instead, and to plan with him means of getting rid of Darnley. Bothwell had such power over her that he induced her even to pardon the assassins of Rizzio. The arrangements for the Christening of the young Prince were entrusted to him, and he was one of the most important people at the ceremony, where the child was named JAMES: Elizabeth being his godmother, though not present on the occasion. A week afterwards, Darnley, who had left Mary and gone to his father's house at Glasgow, being taken ill with the small-pox, she sent her own physician to attend him. But there is reason to apprehend that this was merely a show and a pretence, and that she knew what was doing, when Bothwell within another month proposed to one of the late conspirators against Rizzio, to murder Darnley, 'for that it was the Queen's mind that he should be taken away.' It is certain that on that very day she wrote to her ambassador in France, complaining of him, and yet went immediately to Glasgow, feigning to be very anxious about him, and to love him very much. If she wanted to get him in her power, she succeeded to her heart's content; for she induced him to go back with her to Edinburgh, and to occupy, instead of the palace, a lone house outside the city called the Kirk of Field. Here, he lived for about a week. One Sunday night, she remained with him until ten o'clock, and then left him, to go to Holyrood to be present at an entertainment given in celebration of the marriage of one of her favourite servants. At two o'clock in the morning the city was shaken by a great explosion, and the Kirk of Field was blown to atoms.

Darnley's body was found next day lying under a tree at some distance. How it came there, undisfigured and unscorched by gunpowder, and how this crime came to be so clumsily and strangely committed, it is impossible to discover. The deceitful character of Mary, and the deceitful character of Elizabeth, have rendered almost every part of their joint history uncertain and obscure. But, I fear that Mary was unquestionably a party to her husband's murder, and that this was the revenge she had threatened. The Scotch people universally believed it. Voices cried out in the streets of Edinburgh in the dead of the night, for justice on the murderess. Placards were posted by unknown hands in the public places denouncing Bothwell as the murderer, and the Queen as his accomplice; and, when he afterwards married her (though himself already married), previously making a show of taking her prisoner by force, the indignation of the people knew no bounds. The women particularly are described as having been quite frantic against the Queen, and to have hooted and cried after her in the streets with terrific vehemence.

Such guilty unions seldom prosper. This husband and wife had lived together but a month, when they were separated for ever by the successes of a band of Scotch nobles who associated against them for the protection of the young Prince: whom Bothwell had vainly endeavoured to lay hold of, and whom he would certainly have murdered, if the EARL OF MAR, in whose hands the boy was, had not been firmly and honourably faithful to his trust. Before this angry power, Bothwell fled abroad, where he died, a prisoner and mad, nine miserable years afterwards. Mary being found by the associated lords to deceive them at every turn, was sent a prisoner to Lochleven Castle; which, as it stood in the midst of a lake, could only be approached by boat. Here, one LORD LINDSAY, who was so much of a brute that the nobles would have done better if they had chosen a mere gentleman for their messenger, made her sign her abdication, and appoint Murray, Regent of Scotland. Here, too, Murray saw her in a sorrowing and humbled state.

She had better have remained in the castle of Lochleven, dull prison as it was, with the rippling of the lake against it, and the moving shadows of the water on the room walls; but she could not rest there, and more than once tried to escape. The first time she had nearly succeeded, dressed in the clothes of her own washer-woman, but, putting up her hand to prevent one of the boatmen from lifting her veil, the men suspected her, seeing how white it was, and rowed her back again. A short time afterwards, her fascinating manners enlisted in her cause a boy in the Castle, called the little DOUGLAS, who, while the family were at supper, stole the keys of the great gate, went softly out with the Queen, locked the gate on the outside, and rowed her away across the lake, sinking the keys as they went along. On the opposite shore she was met by another Douglas, and some few lords; and, so accompanied, rode away on horseback to Hamilton, where they raised three thousand men.

Here, she issued a proclamation declaring that the abdication she had signed in her prison was illegal, and requiring the Regent to yield to his lawful Queen. Being a steady soldier, and in no way discomposed although he was without an army, Murray pretended to treat with her, until he had collected a force about half equal to her own, and then he gave her battle. In one quarter of an hour he cut down all her hopes. She had another weary ride on horse-back of sixty long Scotch miles, and took shelter at Dundrennan Abbey, whence she fled for safety to Elizabeth's dominions.

Mary Queen of Scots came to England—to her own ruin, the trouble of the kingdom, and the misery and death of many—in the year one thousand five hundred and sixty-eight. How she left it and the world, nineteen years afterwards, we have now to see.

When Mary Queen of Scots arrived in England, without money and even without any other clothes than those she wore, she wrote to Elizabeth, representing herself as an innocent and injured piece of Royalty, and entreating her assistance to oblige her Scottish subjects to take her back again and obey her. But, as her character was already known in England to be a very different one from what she made it out to be, she was told in answer that she must first clear herself. Made uneasy by this condition, Mary, rather than stay in England, would have gone to Spain, or to France, or would even have gone back to Scotland. But, as her doing either would have been likely to trouble England afresh, it was decided that she should be detained here. She first came to Carlisle, and, after that, was moved about from castle to castle, as was considered necessary; but England she never left again.

After trying very hard to get rid of the necessity of clearing herself, Mary, advised by LORD HERRIES, her best friend in England, agreed to answer the charges against her, if the Scottish noblemen who made them would attend to maintain them before such English noblemen as Elizabeth might appoint for that purpose. Accordingly, such an assembly, under the name of a conference, met, first at York, and afterwards at Hampton Court. In its presence Lord Lennox, Darnley's father, openly charged Mary with the murder of his son; and whatever Mary's friends may now say or write in her behalf, there is no doubt that, when her brother Murray produced against her a casket containing certain guilty letters and verses which he stated to have passed between her and Bothwell, she withdrew from the inquiry. Consequently, it is to be supposed that she was then considered guilty by those who had the best opportunities of judging of the truth, and that the feeling which afterwards arose in her behalf was a very generous but not a very reasonable one.

However, the DUKE OF NORFOLK, an honourable but rather weak nobleman, partly because Mary was captivating, partly because he was ambitious, partly because he was over-persuaded by artful plotters against Elizabeth, conceived a strong idea that he would like to marry the Queen of Scots—though he was a little frightened, too, by the letters in the casket. This idea being secretly encouraged by some of the noblemen of Elizabeth's court, and even by the favourite Earl of Leicester (because it was objected to by other favourites who were his rivals), Mary expressed her approval of it, and the King of France and the King of Spain are supposed to have done the same. It was not so quietly planned, though, but that it came to Elizabeth's ears, who warned the Duke 'to be careful what sort of pillow he was going to lay his head upon.' He made a humble reply at the time; but turned sulky soon afterwards, and, being considered dangerous, was sent to the Tower.

Thus, from the moment of Mary's coming to England she began to be the centre of plots and miseries.

A rise of the Catholics in the north was the next of these, and it was only checked by many executions and much bloodshed. It was followed by a great conspiracy of the Pope and some of the Catholic sovereigns of Europe to depose Elizabeth, place Mary on the throne, and restore the unreformed religion. It is almost impossible to doubt that Mary knew and approved of this; and the Pope himself was so hot in the matter that he issued a bull, in which he openly called Elizabeth the 'pretended Queen' of England, excommunicated her, and excommunicated all her subjects who should continue to obey her. A copy of this miserable paper got into London, and was found one morning publicly posted on the Bishop of London's gate. A great hue and cry being raised, another copy was found in the chamber of a student of Lincoln's Inn, who confessed, being put upon the rack, that he had received it from one JOHN FELTON, a rich gentleman who lived across the Thames, near Southwark. This John Felton, being put upon the rack too, confessed that he had posted the placard on the Bishop's gate. For this offence he was, within four days, taken to St Paul's Churchyard, and there hanged and quartered. As to the Pope's bull, the people by the reformation having thrown off the Pope, did not care much, you may suppose, for the Pope's throwing off them. It was a mere dirty piece of paper, and not half so powerful as a street ballad.

On the very day when Felton was brought to his trial, the poor Duke of Norfolk was released. It would have been well for him if he had kept away from the Tower evermore, and from the snares that had taken him there. But, even while he was in that dismal place he corresponded with Mary, and as soon as he was out of it, he began to plot again. Being discovered in correspondence with the Pope, with a view to a rising in England which should force Elizabeth to consent to his marriage with Mary and to repeal the laws against the Catholics, he was re-committed to the Tower and brought to trial. He was found guilty by the unanimous verdict of the Lords who tried him, and was sentenced to the block.

It is very difficult to make out, at this distance of time, and between opposite accounts, whether Elizabeth really was a humane woman, or desired to appear so, or was fearful of shedding the blood of people of great name who were popular in the country. Twice she commanded and countermanded the execution of this Duke, and it did not take place until five months after his trial. The scaffold was erected on Tower Hill, and there he died like a brave man. He refused to have his eyes bandaged, saying that he was not at all afraid of death; and he admitted the justice of his sentence, and was much regretted by the people.

Although Mary had shrunk at the most important time from disproving her guilt, she was very careful never to do anything that would admit it. All such proposals as were made to her by Elizabeth for her release, required that admission in some form or other, and therefore came to nothing. Moreover, both women being artful and treacherous, and neither ever trusting the other, it was not likely that they could ever make an agreement. So, the Parliament, aggravated by what the Pope had done, made new and strong laws against the spreading of the Catholic religion in England, and declared it treason in any one to say that the Queen and her successors were not the lawful sovereigns of England. It would have done more than this, but for Elizabeth's moderation.

Since the Reformation, there had come to be three great sects of religious people—or people who called themselves so—in England; that is to say, those who belonged to the Reformed Church, those who belonged to the Unreformed Church, and those who were called the Puritans, because they said that they wanted to have everything very pure and plain in all the Church service. These last were for the most part an uncomfortable people, who thought it highly meritorious to dress in a hideous manner, talk through their noses, and oppose all harmless enjoyments. But they were powerful too, and very much in earnest, and they were one and all the determined enemies of the Queen of Scots. The Protestant feeling in England was further strengthened by the tremendous cruelties to which Protestants were exposed in France and in the Netherlands. Scores of thousands of them were put to death in those countries with every cruelty that can be imagined, and at last, in the autumn of the year one thousand five hundred and seventy-two, one of the greatest barbarities ever committed in the world took place at Paris.

It is called in history, THE MASSACRE OF ST BARTHOLOMEW, because it took place on Saint Bartholomew's Eve. The day fell on Saturday the twenty-third of August. On that day all the great leaders of the Protestants (who were there called HUGUENOTS) were assembled together, for the purpose, as was represented to them, of doing honour to the marriage of their chief, the young King of Navarre, with the sister of CHARLES THE NINTH: a miserable young King who then occupied the French throne. This dull creature was made to believe by his mother and other fierce Catholics about him that the Huguenots meant to take his life; and he was persuaded to give secret orders that, on the tolling of a great bell, they should be fallen upon by an overpowering force of armed men, and slaughtered wherever they could be found. When the appointed hour was close at hand, the stupid wretch, trembling from head to foot, was taken into a balcony by his mother to see the atrocious work begun. The moment the bell tolled, the murderers broke forth. During all that night and the two next days, they broke into the houses, fired the houses, shot and stabbed the Protestants, men, women, and children, and flung their bodies into the streets. They were shot at in the streets as they passed along, and their blood ran down the gutters. Upwards of ten thousand Protestants were killed in Paris alone; in all France four or five times that number. To return thanks to Heaven for these diabolical murders, the Pope and his train actually went in public procession at Rome, and as if this were not shame enough for them, they had a medal struck to commemorate the event. But, however comfortable the wholesale murders were to these high authorities, they had not that soothing effect upon the doll-King. I am happy to state that he never knew a moment's peace afterwards; that he was continually crying out that he saw the Huguenots covered with blood and wounds falling dead before him; and that he died within a year, shrieking and yelling and raving to that degree, that if all the Popes who had ever lived had been rolled into one, they would not have afforded His guilty Majesty the slightest consolation.

When the terrible news of the massacre arrived in England, it made a powerful impression indeed upon the people. If they began to run a little wild against the Catholics at about this time, this fearful reason for it, coming so soon after the days of bloody Queen Mary, must be remembered in their excuse. The Court was not quite so honest as the people—but perhaps it sometimes is not. It received the French ambassador, with all the lords and ladies dressed in deep mourning, and keeping a profound silence. Nevertheless, a proposal of marriage which he had made to Elizabeth only two days before the eve of Saint Bartholomew, on behalf of the Duke of Alençon, the French King's brother, a boy of seventeen, still went on; while on the other hand, in her usual crafty way, the Queen secretly supplied the Huguenots with money and weapons.

I must say that for a Queen who made all those fine speeches, of which I have confessed myself to be rather tired, about living and dying a Maiden Queen, Elizabeth was 'going' to be married pretty often. Besides always having some English favourite or other whom she by turns encouraged and swore at and knocked about—for the maiden

Queen was very free with her fists—she held this French Duke off and on through several years. When he at last came over to England, the marriage articles were actually drawn up, and it was settled that the wedding should take place in six weeks. The Queen was then so bent upon it, that she prosecuted a poor Puritan named STUBBS, and a poor bookseller named PAGE, for writing and publishing a pamphlet against it. Their right hands were chopped off for this crime; and poor Stubbs—more loyal than I should have been myself under the circumstances—immediately pulled off his hat with his left hand, and cried, 'God save the Queen!' Stubbs was cruelly treated; for the marriage never took place after all, though the Queen pledged herself to the Duke with a ring from her own finger. He went away, no better than he came, when the courtship had lasted some ten years altogether; and he died a couple of years afterwards, mourned by Elizabeth, who appears to have been really fond of him. It is not much to her credit, for he was a bad enough member of a bad family.

To return to the Catholics. There arose two orders of priests, who were very busy in England,

and who were much dreaded. These were the JESUITS (who were everywhere in all sorts of disguises), and the SEMINARY PRIESTS. The people had a great horror of the first, because they were known to have taught that murder was lawful if it were done with an object of which they approved; and they had a great horror of the second, because they came to teach the old religion, and to be the successors of 'Queen Mary's priests,' as those yet lingering in England were called, when they should die out. The severest laws were made against them, and were most unmercifully executed. Those who sheltered them in their houses often suffered heavily for what was an act of humanity; and the rack, that cruel torture which tore men's limbs asunder, was constantly kept going. What these unhappy men confessed, or what was ever confessed by any one under that agony, must always be received with great doubt, as it is certain that people have frequently owned to the most absurd and impossible crimes to escape such dreadful suffering. But I cannot doubt it to have been proved by papers, that there were many plots, both among the Jesuits, and with France, and with Scotland, and with Spain, for the destruction of Queen Elizabeth, for the placing of Mary on the throne, and for the revival of the old religion.

If the English people were too ready to believe in plots, there were, as I have said, good reasons for it. When the massacre of Saint Bartholomew was yet fresh in their recollection, a great Protestant Dutch hero, the PRINCE OF ORANGE, was shot by an assassin, who confessed that he had been kept and trained for the purpose in a college of Jesuits. The Dutch, in this surprise and distress, offered to make Elizabeth their sovereign, but she declined the honour, and sent them a small army instead, under the command of the Earl of Leicester, who, although a capital Court favourite, was not much of a general. He did so little in Holland, that his campaign there would probably have been forgotten, but for its occasioning the death of one of the best writers, the best knights, and the best gentlemen, of that or any age. This was SIR PHILIP SIDNEY, who was wounded by a musket ball in the thigh as he mounted a fresh horse, after having had his own killed under him. He had to ride back wounded, a long distance, and was very faint with fatigue and loss of blood, when some water, for which he had eagerly asked, was handed to him. But he was so good and gentle even then, that seeing a poor badly wounded common soldier lying on the ground, looking at the water with longing eyes, he said, 'Thy necessity is greater than mine,' and gave it up to him. This touching action of a noble heart is perhaps as well known as any incident in history—it is as famous far and wide as the blood-stained Tower of London, with its axe, and block, and murders out of number. So delightful is an act of true humanity, and so glad are mankind to remember it.

At home, intelligence of plots began to thicken every day. I suppose the people never did live under such continual terrors as those by which they were possessed now, of Catholic risings, and burnings, and poisonings, and I don't know what. Still, we must always remember that they lived near and close to awful realities of that kind, and that with their experience it was not difficult to believe in any enormity. The government had the same fear, and did not take the best means of discovering the truth—for, besides torturing the suspected, it employed paid spies, who will always lie for their own profit. It even made some of the conspiracies it brought to light, by sending false letters to disaffected people, inviting them to join in pretended plots, which they too readily did.

But, one great real plot was at length discovered, and it ended the career of Mary, Queen of Scots. A seminary priest named BALLARD, and a Spanish soldier named SAVAGE, set on and encouraged by certain French priests, imparted a design to one ANTONY BABINGTON—a gentleman of fortune in Derbyshire, who had been for some time a secret agent of Mary's—for murdering the Queen. Babington then confided the scheme to some other Catholic gentlemen who were his friends, and they joined in it heartily. They were vain, weak-headed young men, ridiculously confident, and preposterously proud of their plan; for they got a gimcrack painting made, of the six choice spirits who were to murder Elizabeth, with Babington in an attitude for the centre figure. Two of their number, however, one of whom was a priest, kept Elizabeth's wisest minister, SIR FRANCIS WALSINGHAM, acquainted with the whole project from the first. The conspirators were completely deceived to the final point, when Babington gave Savage, because he was shabby, a ring from his finger, and some money from his purse, wherewith to buy himself new clothes in which to kill the Queen. Walsingham, having then full evidence against the whole band, and two letters of Mary's besides, resolved to seize them. Suspecting something wrong, they stole out of the city, one by one, and hid themselves in St John's Wood, and other places which really were hiding places then; but they were all taken, and all executed. When they were seized, a gentleman was sent from Court to inform Mary of the fact, and of her being involved in the discovery. Her friends have complained that she was kept in very hard and severe custody. It does not appear very likely, for she was going out a hunting that very morning.

Queen Elizabeth had been warned long ago, by one in France who had good information of what was secretly doing, that in holding Mary alive, she held 'the wolf who would devour her.' The Bishop of London had, more lately, given the Queen's favourite minister the advice in writing, 'forthwith to cut off the Scottish Queen's head.' The question now was, what to do with her? The Earl of Leicester wrote a little note home from Holland, recommending that she should be quietly poisoned; that noble favourite having accustomed his mind, it is possible, to remedies of that nature. His black advice, however, was disregarded, and she was brought to trial at Fotheringay Castle in Northamptonshire, before a tribunal of forty, composed of both religions. There, and in the Star Chamber at Westminster, the trial lasted a fortnight. She defended herself with great ability, but could only deny the confessions that had been made by Babington and others; could only call her own letters, produced against her by her own secretaries, forgeries; and, in short, could only deny everything. She was found guilty, and declared to have incurred the penalty of death. The Parliament met, approved the sentence, and prayed the Queen to have it executed. The Queen replied that she requested them to consider whether no means could be found of saving Mary's life without endangering her own. The Parliament rejoined, No; and the citizens illuminated their houses and lighted bonfires, in token of their joy that all these plots and troubles were to be ended by the death of the Queen of Scots.

She, feeling sure that her time was now come, wrote a letter to the Queen of England, making three entreaties; first, that she might be buried in France; secondly, that she might not be executed in secret, but before her servants and some others; thirdly, that after her death, her servants should not be molested, but should be suffered to go home with the legacies she left them. It was an affecting letter, and Elizabeth shed tears over it, but sent no answer. Then came a special ambassador from France, and another from Scotland, to intercede for Mary's life; and then the nation began to clamour, more and more, for her death.

What the real feelings or intentions of Elizabeth were, can never be known now; but I strongly suspect her of only wishing one thing more than Mary's death, and that was to keep free of the blame of it. On the first of February, one thousand five hundred and eighty-seven, Lord Burleigh having drawn out the warrant for the execution, the Queen sent to the secretary DAVISON to bring it to her, that she might sign it: which she did. Next day, when Davison told her it was sealed, she angrily asked him why such haste was necessary? Next day but one, she joked about it, and swore a little. Again, next day but one, she seemed to complain that it was not yet done, but still she would not be plain with those about her. So, on the seventh, the Earls of Kent and Shrewsbury, with the Sheriff of Northamptonshire, came with the warrant to Fotheringay, to tell the Queen of Scots to prepare for death.

When those messengers of ill omen were gone, Mary made a frugal supper, drank to her servants, read over her will, went to bed, slept for some hours, and then arose and passed the remainder of the night saying prayers. In the morning she dressed herself in her best clothes; and, at eight o'clock when the sheriff came for her to her chapel, took leave of her servants who were there assembled praying with her, and went down-stairs, carrying a Bible in one hand and a crucifix in the other. Two of her women and four of her men were allowed to be present in the hall; where a low scaffold, only two feet from the ground, was erected and covered with black; and where the executioner from the Tower, and his assistant, stood, dressed in black velvet. The hall was full of people. While the sentence was being read she sat upon a stool; and, when it was finished, she again denied her guilt, as she had done before. The Earl of Kent and the Dean of Peterborough, in their

Protestant zeal, made some very unnecessary speeches to her; to which she replied that she died in the Catholic religion, and they need not trouble themselves about that matter. When her head and neck were uncovered by the executioners, she said that she had not been used to be undressed by such hands, or before so much company. Finally, one of her women fastened a cloth over her face, and she laid her neck upon the block, and repeated more than once in Latin, 'Into thy hands, O Lord, I commend my spirit!' Some say her head was struck off in two blows, some say in three. However that be, when it was held up, streaming with blood, the real hair beneath the false hair she had long worn was seen to be as grey as that of a woman of seventy, though she was at that time only in her forty-sixth year. All her beauty was gone.

But she was beautiful enough to her little dog, who cowered under her dress, frightened, when she went upon the scaffold, and who lay down beside her headless body when all her earthly sorrows were over.

On its being formally made known to Elizabeth that the sentence had been executed on the Queen of Scots, she showed the utmost grief and rage, drove her favourites from her with violent indignation, and sent Davison to the Tower; from which place he was only released in the end by paying an immense fine which completely ruined him. Elizabeth not only over-acted her part in making these pretences, but most basely reduced to poverty one of her faithful servants for no other fault than obeying her commands.

James, King of Scotland, Mary's son, made a show likewise of being very angry on the occasion; but he was a pensioner of England to the amount of five thousand pounds a year, and he had known very little of his mother, and he possibly regarded her as the murderer of his father, and he soon took it quietly.

Philip, King of Spain, however, threatened to do greater things than ever had been done yet, to set up the Catholic religion and punish Protestant England. Elizabeth, hearing that he and the Prince of Parma were making great preparations for this purpose, in order to be beforehand with them sent out ADMIRAL DRAKE (a famous navigator, who had sailed about the world, and had already brought great plunder from Spain) to the port of Cadiz, where he burnt a hundred vessels full of stores. This great loss obliged the Spaniards to put off the invasion for a year; but it was none the less formidable for that, amounting to one hundred and thirty ships, nineteen thousand soldiers, eight thousand sailors, two thousand slaves, and between two and three thousand great guns. England was not idle in making ready to resist this great force. All the men between sixteen years old and sixty, were trained and drilled; the national fleet of ships (in number only thirty-four at first) was enlarged by public contributions and by private ships, fitted out by noblemen; the city of London, of its own accord, furnished double the number of ships and men that it was required to provide; and, if ever the national spirit was up in England, it was up all through the country to resist the Spaniards. Some of the Queen's advisers were for seizing the principal English Catholics, and putting them to death; but the Queen—who, to her honour, used to say, that she would never believe any ill of her subjects, which a parent would not believe of her own children—rejected the advice, and only confined a few of those who were the most suspected, in the fens in Lincolnshire. The great body of Catholics deserved this confidence;

for they behaved most loyally, nobly, and bravely.

So, with all England firing up like one strong, angry man, and with both sides of the Thames fortified, and with the soldiers under arms, and with the sailors in their ships, the country waited for the coming of the proud Spanish fleet, which was called THE INVINCIBLE ARMADA. The Queen herself, riding in armour on a white horse, and the Earl of Essex and the Earl of Leicester holding her bridle rein, made a brave speech to the troops at Tilbury Fort opposite Gravesend, which was received with such enthusiasm as is seldom known. Then came the Spanish Armada into the English Channel, sailing along in the form of a half moon, of such great size that it was seven miles broad. But the English were quickly upon it, and woe then to all the Spanish ships that dropped a little out of the half moon, for the English took them instantly! And it soon appeared that the great Armada was anything but invincible, for on a summer night, bold Drake sent eight blazing fire-ships right into the midst of it. In terrible consternation the Spaniards tried to get out to sea, and so became dispersed; the English pursued them at a great advantage; a storm came on, and drove the Spaniards among rocks and shoals; and the swift end of the Invincible fleet was, that it lost thirty great ships and ten thousand men, and, defeated and disgraced, sailed home again. Being afraid to go by the English Channel, it sailed all round Scotland and Ireland; some of the ships getting cast away on the latter coast in bad weather, the Irish, who were a kind of savages, plundered those vessels and killed their crews. So ended this great attempt to invade and conquer England. And I think it will be a long time before any other invincible fleet coming to England with the same object, will fare much better than the Spanish Armada.

Though the Spanish king had had this bitter taste of English bravery, he was so little the wiser for it, as still to entertain his old designs, and even to conceive the absurd idea of placing his daughter on the English throne. But the Earl of Essex, SIR WALTER RALEIGH, SIR THOMAS HOWARD, and some other distinguished leaders, put to sea from Plymouth, entered the port of Cadiz once more, obtained a complete victory over the shipping assembled there, and got possession of the town. In obedience to the Queen's express instructions, they behaved with great humanity; and the principal loss of the Spaniards was a vast sum of money which they had to pay for ransom. This was one of many gallant achievements on the sea, effected in this reign. Sir Walter Raleigh himself, after marrying a maid of honour and giving offence to the Maiden Queen thereby, had already sailed to South America in search of gold.

The Earl of Leicester was now dead, and so was Sir Thomas Walsingham, whom Lord Burleigh was soon to follow. The principal favourite was the EARL OF ESSEX, a spirited and handsome man, a favourite with the people too as well as with the Queen, and possessed of many admirable qualities. It was much debated at Court whether there should be peace with Spain or no, and he was very urgent for war. He also tried hard to have his own way in the appointment of a deputy to govern in Ireland. One day, while this question was in dispute, he hastily took offence, and turned his back upon the Queen; as a gentle reminder of which impropriety, the Queen gave him a tremendous box on the ear, and told him to go to the devil. He went home instead, and did not reappear at Court for half a year or so, when he and the Queen were reconciled, though never (as some suppose) thoroughly.

From this time the fate of the Earl of Essex and that of the Queen seemed to be blended together. The Irish were still perpetually quarrelling and fighting among themselves, and he went over to Ireland as Lord Lieutenant, to the great joy of his enemies (Sir Walter Raleigh among the rest), who were glad to have so dangerous a rival far off. Not being by any means successful there, and knowing that his enemies would take advantage of that circumstance to injure him with the Queen, he came home again, though against her orders. The Queen being taken by surprise when he appeared before her, gave him her hand to kiss, and he was overjoyed—though it was not a very lovely hand by this time—but in the course of the same day she ordered him to confine himself to his room, and two or three days afterwards had him taken into custody. With the same sort of caprice—and as capricious an old woman she now was, as ever wore a crown or a head either—she sent him broth from her own table on his falling ill from anxiety, and cried about him.

He was a man who could find comfort and

occupation in his books, and he did so for a time; not the least happy time, I dare say, of his life. But it happened unfortunately for him, that he held a monopoly in sweet wines: which means that nobody could sell them without purchasing his permission. This right, which was only for a term, expiring, he applied to have it renewed. The Queen refused, with the rather strong observation—but she *did* make strong observations—that an unruly beast must be stinted in his food. Upon this, the angry Earl, who had been already deprived of many offices, thought himself in danger of complete ruin, and turned against the Queen, whom he called a vain old woman who had grown as crooked in her mind as she had in her figure. These uncomplimentary expressions the ladies of the Court immediately snapped up and carried to the Queen, whom they did not put in a better temper, you may believe. The same Court ladies, when they had beautiful dark hair of their own, used to wear false red hair, to be like the Queen. So they were not very high-spirited ladies, however high in rank.

The worst object of the Earl of Essex, and some friends of his who used to meet at LORD

SOUTHAMPTON's house, was to obtain possession of the Queen, and oblige her by force to dismiss her ministers and change her favourites. On Saturday the seventh of February, one thousand six hundred and one, the council suspecting this, summoned the Earl to come before them. He, pretending to be ill, declined; it was then settled among his friends, that as the next day would be Sunday, when many of the citizens usually assembled at the Cross by St Paul's Cathedral, he should make one bold effort to induce them to rise and follow him to the Palace.

So, on the Sunday morning, he and a small body of adherents started out of his house—Essex House by the Strand, with steps to the river—having first shut up in it, as prisoners, some members of the council who came to examine him—and hurried into the City with the Earl at their head crying out 'For the Queen! For the Queen! A plot is laid for my life!' No one heeded them, however, and when they came to St Paul's there were no citizens there. In the meantime the prisoners at Essex House had been released by one of the Earl's own friends; he had been promptly proclaimed a traitor in the City itself; and the streets were barricaded with carts and guarded by soldiers. The Earl got back to his house by water, with difficulty, and after an attempt to defend his house against the troops and cannon by which it was soon surrounded, gave himself up that night. He was brought to trial on the nineteenth, and found guilty; on the twenty-fifth, he was executed on Tower Hill, where he died, at thirty-four years old, both courageously and penitently. His step-father suffered with him. His enemy, Sir Walter Raleigh, stood near the scaffold all the time— but not so near it as we shall see him stand, before we finish his history.

In this case, as in the cases of the Duke of Norfolk and Mary Queen of Scots, the Queen had commanded, and countermanded, and again commanded, the execution. It is probable that the death of her young and gallant favourite in the prime of his good qualities, was never off her mind afterwards, but she held out, the same vain, obstinate and capricious woman, for another year. Then she danced before her Court on a state occasion—and cut, I should think, a mighty ridiculous figure, doing so in an immense ruff, stomacher and wig, at seventy years old. For another year still, she held out, but, without any more dancing, and as a moody, sorrowful, broken creature. At last, on the tenth of March, one thousand six hundred and three, having been ill of a very bad cold, and made worse by the death of the Countess of Nottingham who was her intimate friend, she fell into a stupor and was supposed to be dead. She recovered her consciousness, however, and then nothing would induce her to go to bed; for she said that she knew that if she did, she should never get up again. There she lay for ten days, on cushions on the floor, without any food, until the Lord Admiral got her into bed at last, partly by persuasions and partly by main force. When they asked her who should succeed her, she replied that her seat had been the seat of Kings, and that she would have for her successor, 'No rascal's son, but a King's.' Upon this, the lords present stared at one another, and took the liberty of asking whom she meant; to which she replied, 'Whom should I mean, but our cousin of Scotland!' This was on the twenty-third of March. They asked her once again that day, after she was speechless, whether she was still in the same mind? She struggled up in bed, and joined her hands over her head in the form of a crown, as the only reply she could make. At three o'clock next morning, she very quietly died, in the forty-fifth year of her reign.

That reign had been a glorious one, and is made for ever memorable by the distinguished men who flourished in it. Apart from the great voyagers, statesmen, and scholars, whom it produced, the names of BACON, SPENSER, and SHAKESPEARE, will always be remembered with pride and veneration by the civilised world, and will always impart (though with no great reason, perhaps) some portion of their lustre to the name of Elizabeth herself. It was a great reign for discovery, for commerce, and for English enterprise and spirit in general. It was a great reign for the Protestant religion and for the Reformation which made England free. The Queen was very popular, and in her progresses, or journeys about her dominions, was everywhere received with the liveliest joy. I think the truth is, that she was not half so good as she has been made out, and not half so bad as she has been made out. She had her fine qualities, but she was coarse, capricious, and treacherous, and had all the faults of an excessively vain young woman long after she was an old one. On the whole, she had a great deal too much of her father in her, to please me.

Many improvements and luxuries were introduced in the course of these five-and-forty years in the general manner of living; but cock-fighting, bull-baiting, and bear-baiting, were still the national amusements; and a coach was so rarely seen, and was such an ugly and cumbersome affair when it was seen, that even the Queen herself, on many high occasions, rode on horseback on a pillion behind the Lord Chancellor.

England under James the First

'Our cousin of Scotland' was ugly, awkward, and shuffling both in mind and person. His tongue was much too large for his mouth, his legs were much too weak for his body, and his dull goggle-eyes stared and rolled like an idiot's. He was cunning, covetous, wasteful, idle, drunken, greedy, dirty, cowardly, a great swearer, and the most conceited man on earth. His figure—what is commonly called rickety from his birth—presented a most ridiculous appearance, dressed in thick padded clothes, as a safeguard against being stabbed (of which he lived in continual fear), of a grass-green colour from head to foot, with a hunting-horn dangling at his side instead of a sword, and his hat and feather sticking over one eye, or hanging on the back of his head, as he happened to toss it on. He used to loll on the necks of his favourite courtiers, and slobber their faces, and kiss and pinch their cheeks; and the greatest favourite he ever had, used to sign himself in his letters to his royal master, His Majesty's 'dog and slave,' and used to address his majesty as 'his Sowship.' His majesty was the worst rider ever seen, and thought himself the best. He was one of the most impertinent talkers (in the broadest Scotch) ever heard, and boasted of being unanswerable in all manner of argument. He wrote some of the most wearisome treatises ever read—among others, a book upon witchcraft, in which he was a devout believer—and thought himself a prodigy of authorship. He thought, and wrote, and said, that a king had a right to make and unmake what laws he pleased, and ought to be accountable to nobody on earth. This is the plain, true character of the personage whom the greatest men about the court praised and flattered to that degree, that I doubt if there be anything much more shameful in the annals of human nature.

He came to the English throne with great ease. The miseries of a disputed succession had been felt so long, and so dreadfully, that he was proclaimed within a few hours of Elizabeth's death, and was accepted by the nation, even without being asked to give any pledge that he would govern well, or that he would redress crying grievances. He took a month to come from Edinburgh to London; and, by way of exercising his new power, hanged a pickpocket on the journey without any trial, and knighted everybody he could lay hold of. He made two hundred knights before he got to his palace in London, and seven hundred before he had been in it three months. He also shovelled sixty-two new peers into the House of Lords—and there was a pretty large sprinkling of Scotchmen among them, you may believe.

His Sowship's prime Minister, CECIL (for I cannot do better than call his majesty what his favourite called him), was the enemy of Sir Walter Raleigh, and also of Sir Walter's political friend, LORD COBHAM; and his Sowship's first trouble was a plot originated by these two, and entered into by some others, with the old object of seizing the King and keeping him in imprisonment until he should change his ministers. There were Catholic priests in the plot, and there were Puritan noblemen too; for, although the Catholics and Puritans were strongly opposed to each other, they united at this time against his Sowship, because they knew that he had a design against both, after pretending to be friendly to each; this design being to have only one high and convenient form of the Protestant religion, which everybody should be bound to belong to, whether they liked it or not. This plot was mixed up with another, which may or may not have had some reference to placing on the throne, at some time, the LADY ARABELLA STUART; whose misfortune it was, to be the daughter of the younger brother of his Sowship's father, but who was quite innocent of any part in the scheme. Sir Walter Raleigh was accused on the confession of Lord Cobham—a miserable creature, who said one thing at one time, and another thing at another time, and could be relied upon in nothing. The trial of Sir Walter Raleigh lasted from eight in the morning until nearly midnight; he defended himself with such eloquence, genius, and spirit against all accusations, and against the insults of COKE, the Attorney-General—who, according to the custom of the time, foully abused him—that those who went there detesting the prisoner, came away admiring him, and declaring that anything so wonderful and so captivating was never heard. He was found guilty, nevertheless, and sentenced to death. Execution was deferred, and he was taken to the Tower. The two Catholic priests, less fortunate, were executed with the usual atrocity; and Lord Cobham and two others were pardoned on the scaffold. His Sowship thought it wonderfully knowing in him to surprise the people by pardoning these three at the very block; but, blundering, and bungling, as usual, he had very nearly over-reached himself. For, the messenger on horseback who brought the pardon, came so late, that he was pushed to the outside of the crowd, and was obliged to shout and roar out what he came for. The miserable Cobham did not gain much by being spared that day. He lived, both as a prisoner and a beggar, utterly despised, and miserably poor, for thirteen years, and then died in an old outhouse belonging to one of his former servants.

This plot got rid of, and Sir Walter Raleigh safely shut up in the Tower, his Sowship held a great dispute with the Puritans on their presenting a petition to him, and had it all his own way—not so very wonderful, as he would talk continually, and would not hear anybody else—and filled the Bishops with admiration. It was comfortably settled that there was to be only one form of religion, and that all men were to think exactly alike. But, although this was arranged two centuries and a half ago, and although the arrangement was supported by much fining and imprisonment, I do not find that it is quite successful, even yet.

His Sowship, having that uncommonly high opinion of himself as a king, had a very low opinion of Parliament as a power that audaciously wanted to control him. When he called his first Parliament after he had been king a year, he accordingly thought he would take pretty high ground with them, and told them that he commanded them 'as an absolute king.' The Parliament thought those strong words, and saw the necessity of upholding their authority. His Sowship had three children: Prince Henry, Prince Charles, and the Princess Elizabeth. It would have been well for one of these, and we shall too soon see which, if he had learnt a little wisdom concerning Parliaments from his father's obstinacy.

Now, the people still labouring under their old dread of the Catholic religion, this Parliament revived and strengthened the severe laws against it. And this so angered ROBERT CATESBY, a restless Catholic gentleman of an old family, that he formed one of the most desperate and terrible designs ever conceived in the mind of man; no less a scheme than the Gunpowder Plot.

His object was, when the King, lords, and commons, should be assembled at the next opening of Parliament, to blow them up, one and all, with a great mine of gunpowder. The first person to whom he confided this horrible idea was THOMAS WINTER, a Worcestershire gentleman who had served in the army abroad, and had been secretly employed in Catholic projects. While Winter was yet undecided, and when he had gone over to the Netherlands, to learn from the Spanish Ambassador there whether there was any hope of Catholics being relieved through the intercession of the King of Spain with his Sowship, he found at Ostend a tall, dark, daring man, whom he had known when they were both soldiers abroad, and whose name was GUIDO—or GUY—FAWKES. Resolved to join the plot, he proposed it to this man, knowing him to be the man for any desperate deed, and they two came back to England together. Here, they admitted two other conspirators: THOMAS PERCY, related to the Earl of Northumberland, and JOHN WRIGHT, his brother-in-law. All these met together in a solitary house in the open fields which were then near Clement's Inn, now a closely blocked-up part of London; and when they had all taken a great oath of secrecy, Catesby told the rest what his plan was. They then went up-stairs into a garret, and received the Sacrament from FATHER GERARD, a Jesuit, who is said not to have known actually of the Gunpowder Plot, but who, I think, must have had his suspicions that there was something desperate afoot.

Percy was a Gentleman Pensioner, and as he had occasional duties to perform about the Court, then kept at Whitehall, there would be nothing suspicious in his living at Westminster. So, having looked well about him, and having found a house to let, the back of which joined the Parliament House, he hired it of a person named FERRIS, for the purpose of undermining the wall. Having got possession of this house, the conspirators hired another on the Lambeth side of the Thames, which they used as a storehouse for wood, gunpowder, and other combustible matters. These were to be removed at night (and afterwards were removed), bit by bit, to the house at Westminster; and, that there might be some trusty person to keep watch over the Lambeth stores, they admitted another conspirator, by name ROBERT KAY, a very poor Catholic gentleman.

All these arrangements had been made some months, and it was a dark, wintry, December night, when the conspirators, who had been in the meantime dispersed to avoid observation, met in the house at Westminster, and began to dig. They had laid in a good stock of eatables, to avoid going in and out, and they dug and dug with great ardour. But, the wall being tremendously thick, and the work very severe, they took into their plot CHRISTOPHER WRIGHT, a younger brother of John Wright, that they might have a new pair of hands to help. And Christopher Wright fell to like a fresh man, and they dug and dug by night and by day, and Fawkes stood sentinel all the time. And if any man's heart seemed to fail him at all, Fawkes said, 'Gentlemen, we have abundance of powder and shot here, and there is no fear of our being taken alive, even if discovered.' The same Fawkes, who, in the capacity of sentinel, was always prowling about, soon picked up the intelligence that the King had prorogued the Parliament again, from the seventh of February, the day first fixed upon, until the third of October. When the conspirators knew this, they agreed to separate until after the Christmas holidays, and to take no notice of each other in the meanwhile, and never to write letters to one another on any account. So, the house in Westminster was shut up again, and I suppose the neighbours thought that those strange-looking men who lived there so gloomily, and went out so seldom, were gone away to have a merry Christmas somewhere.

It was the beginning of February, sixteen hundred and five, when Catesby met his fellow-conspirators again at this Westminster house. He had now admitted three more: JOHN GRANT, a Warwickshire gentleman of a melancholy temper, who lived in a doleful house near Stratford-upon-Avon, with a frowning wall all round it, and a deep moat; ROBERT WINTER, eldest brother of Thomas; and Catesby's own servant, THOMAS BATES, who, Catesby thought, had had some suspicion of what his master was about. These three had all suffered more or less for their religion in Elizabeth's time. And now, they all began to dig again, and they dug and dug by night and by day.

They found it dismal work alone there, underground, with such a fearful secret on their minds, and so many murders before them. They were filled with wild fancies. Sometimes, they thought they heard a great bell tolling, deep down in the earth under the Parliament House; sometimes, they thought they heard low voices muttering about the Gunpowder Plot; once in the morning, they really did hear a great rumbling noise over their heads, as they dug and sweated in their mine. Every man stopped and looked aghast at his neighbour, wondering what had happened, when that bold prowler, Fawkes, who had been out to look, came in and told them that it was only a dealer in coals who had occupied a cellar under the Parliament House, removing his stock in trade to some other place. Upon this, the conspirators, who with all their digging and digging had not yet dug through the tremendously thick wall, changed their plan; hired that cellar, which was directly under the House of Lords; put six-and-thirty barrels of gunpowder in it, and covered them over with fagots and coals. Then they all dispersed again till September, when the following new conspirators were admitted: SIR EDWARD BAYNHAM, of Gloucestershire; SIR EVERARD DIGBY, of Rutlandshire; AMBROSE ROOKWOOD, of Suffolk; FRANCIS TRESHAM, of Northamptonshire. Most of these were rich, and were to assist the plot, some with money and some with horses on which the conspirators were to ride through the country and rouse the Catholics after the Parliament should be blown into air.

Parliament being again prorogued from the third of October to the fifth of November, and the conspirators being uneasy lest their design should have been found out, Thomas Winter said he would go up into the House of Lords on the day of the prorogation, and see how matters looked. Nothing could be better. The unconscious Commissioners were walking about and talking to one another, just over the six-and-thirty barrels of gunpowder. He came back and told the rest so, and they went on with their preparations. They hired a ship, and kept it ready in the Thames, in which Fawkes was to sail for Flanders after firing with a slow match the train that was to explode the powder. A number of Catholic gentlemen not in the secret, were invited, on pretence of a hunting party, to meet Sir Everard Digby at Dunchurch on the fatal day, that they might be ready to act together. And now all was ready.

But, now, the great wickedness and danger which had been all along at the bottom of this wicked plot, began to show itself. As the fifth of November drew near, most of the conspirators, remembering that they had friends and relations who would be in the House of Lords that day, felt some natural relenting, and a wish to warn them to keep away. They were not much comforted by Catesby's declaring that in such a cause he would blow up his own son. LORD MOUNTEAGLE, Tresham's brother-in-law, was certain to be in the house; and when Tresham found that he could not prevail upon the rest to devise any means of sparing their friends, he wrote a mysterious letter to this lord and left it at his lodging in the dusk, urging him to keep away from the opening of

Parliament, 'since God and man had concurred to punish the wickedness of the times.' It contained the words 'that the Parliament should receive a terrible blow, and yet should not see who hurt them.' And it added, 'the danger is past, as soon as you have burnt the letter.'

The ministers and courtiers made out that his Sowship, by a direct miracle from Heaven, found out what this letter meant. The truth is, that they were not long (as few men would be) in finding out for themselves; and it was decided to let the conspirators alone, until the very day before the opening of Parliament. That the conspirators had their fears, is certain; for, Tresham himself said before them all, that they were every one dead men; and, although even he did not take flight, there is reason to suppose that he had warned other persons besides Lord Mounteagle. However, they were all firm; and Fawkes, who was a man of iron, went down every day and night to keep watch in the cellar as usual. He was there about two in the afternoon of the fourth, when the Lord Chamberlain and Lord Mounteagle threw open the door and looked in. 'Who are you, friend?' said they. 'Why,' said Fawkes, 'I am Mr Percy's servant, and am looking after his store of fuel here.' 'Your master has laid in a pretty good store,' they returned, and shut the door, and went away. Fawkes, upon this, posted off to the other conspirators to tell them all was quiet, and went back and shut himself up in the dark, black cellar again, where he heard the bell go twelve o'clock and usher in the fifth of November. About two hours afterwards, he slowly opened the door, and came out to look about him, in his old prowling way. He was instantly seized and bound, by a party of soldiers under SIR THOMAS KNEVETT. He had a watch upon him, some touchwood, some tinder, some slow matches; and there was a dark lantern with a candle in it, lighted, behind the door. He had his boots and spurs on—to ride to the ship, I suppose—and it was well for the soldiers that they took him so suddenly. If they had left him but a moment's time to light a match, he certainly would have tossed it in among the powder, and blown up himself and them.

They took him to the King's bed-chamber first of all, and there the King (causing him to be held very tight, and keeping a good way off), asked him how he could have the heart to intend to destroy so many innocent people? 'Because,' said Guy Fawkes, 'desperate diseases need desperate remedies.' To a little Scotch favourite, with a face like a terrier, who asked him (with no particular wisdom) why he had collected so much gunpowder, he replied, because he had meant to blow Scotchmen back to Scotland, and it would take a deal of powder to do that. Next day he was carried to the Tower, but would make no confession. Even after being horribly tortured, he confessed nothing that the Government did not already know; though he must have been in a fearful state—as his signature, still preserved, in contrast with his natural handwriting before he was put upon the dreadful rack, most frightfully shows. Bates, a very different man, soon said the Jesuits had had to do with the plot, and probably, under the torture, would as readily have said anything. Tresham, taken and put in the Tower too, made confessions and unmade them, and died of an illness that was heavy upon him. Rookwood, who had stationed relays of his own horses all the way to Dunchurch, did not mount to escape until the middle of the day, when the news of the plot was all over London. On the road, he came up with the two Wrights, Catesby, and Percy;

and they all galloped together into Northamptonshire. Thence to Dunchurch, where they found the proposed party assembled. Finding, however, that there had been a plot, and that it had been discovered, the party disappeared in the course of the night, and left them alone with Sir Everard Digby. Away they all rode again, through Warwickshire and Worcestershire, to a house called Holbeach, on the borders of Staffordshire. They tried to raise the Catholics on their way, but were indignantly driven off by them. All this time they were hotly pursued by the sheriff of Worcester, and a fast increasing concourse of riders. At last, resolving to defend themselves at Holbeach, they shut themselves up in the house, and put some wet powder before the fire to dry. But it blew up, and Catesby was singed and blackened, and almost killed, and some of the others were sadly hurt. Still, knowing that they must die, they resolved to die there, and with only their swords in their hands appeared at the windows to be shot at by the sheriff and his assistants. Catesby said to Thomas Winter, after Thomas had been hit in the right arm which dropped powerless by his side, 'Stand by me, Tom, and we will die together!'—which they did, being shot through the body by two bullets from one gun. John Wright, and Christopher Wright, and Percy, were also shot. Rookwood and Digby were taken: the former with a broken arm and a wound in his body too.

It was the fifteenth of January, before the trial of Guy Fawkes, and such of the other conspirators as were left alive, came on. They were all found guilty, all hanged, drawn, and quartered: some, in St Paul's Churchyard, on the top of Ludgate-hill; some, before the Parliament House. A Jesuit priest, named HENRY GARNET, to whom the dreadful design was said to have been communicated, was taken and tried; and two of his servants, as well as a poor priest who was taken with him, were tortured without mercy. He himself was not tortured, but was surrounded in the Tower by tamperers and traitors, and so was made unfairly to convict himself out of his own mouth. He said, upon his trial, that he had done all he could to prevent the deed, and that he could not make public what had been told him in confession—though I am afraid he knew of the plot in other ways. He was found guilty and executed, after a manful defence, and the Catholic Church made a saint of him; some rich and powerful persons, who had had nothing to do with the project, were fined and imprisoned for it by the Star Chamber; the Catholics, in general, who had recoiled with horror from the idea of the infernal contrivance, were unjustly put under more severe laws than before; and this was the end of the Gunpowder Plot.

His Sowship would pretty willingly, I think, have blown the House of Commons into the air himself; for, his dread and jealousy of it knew no bounds all through his reign. When he was hard pressed for money he was obliged to order it to meet, as he could get no money without it; and when it asked him first to abolish some of the monopolies in necessaries of life which were a great grievance to the people, and to redress other public wrongs, he flew into a rage and got rid of it again. At one time he wanted it to consent to the Union of England with Scotland, and quarrelled about that. At another time it wanted him to put down a most infamous Church abuse, called the High Commission Court, and he quarrelled with it about that. At another time it entreated him not to be quite so fond of his archbishops and bishops who made speeches in his praise too awful to be related, but to have some little consideration for the poor Puritan clergy who were persecuted for preaching in their own way, and not according to the archbishops and bishops; and they quarrelled about that. In short, what with hating the House of Commons, and pretending not to hate it; and what with now sending some of its members who opposed him, to Newgate or to the Tower, and now telling the rest that they must not presume to make speeches about the public affairs which could not possibly concern them; and what with cajoling, and bullying, and fighting, and being frightened; the House of Commons was the plague of his Sowship's existence. It was pretty firm, however, in maintaining its rights, and insisting that the Parliament should make the laws, and not the King by his own single proclamations (which he tried hard to do); and his Sowship was so often distressed for money, in consequence, that he sold every sort of title and public office as if they were merchandise, and even invented a new dignity called a Baronetcy, which anybody could buy for a thousand pounds.

These disputes with his Parliaments, and his hunting, and his drinking, and his lying in bed—

for he was a great sluggard—occupied his Sowship pretty well. The rest of his time he chiefly passed in hugging and slobbering his favourites. The first of these was SIR PHILIP HERBERT, who had no knowledge whatever, except of dogs, and horses, and hunting, but whom he soon made EARL OF MONTGOMERY. The next, and a much more famous one, was ROBERT CARR, or KER (for it is not certain which was his right name), who came from the Border country, and whom he soon made VISCOUNT ROCHESTER, and afterwards, EARL OF SOMERSET. The way in which his Sowship doted on this handsome young man, is even more odious to think of, than the way in which the really great men of England condescended to bow down before him. The favourite's great friend was a certain SIR THOMAS OVERBURY, who wrote his love-letters for him, and assisted him in the duties of his many high places, which his own ignorance prevented him from discharging. But this same Sir Thomas having just manhood enough to dissuade the favourite from a wicked marriage with the beautiful Countess of Essex, who was to get a divorce from her husband for the purpose, the said Countess, in her rage, got Sir

Thomas put into the Tower, and there poisoned him. Then the favourite and this bad woman were publicly married by the King's pet bishop, with as much to-do and rejoicing, as if he had been the best man, and she the best woman, upon the face of the earth.

But, after a longer sunshine than might have been expected—of seven years or so, that is to say—another handsome young man started up and eclipsed the Earl of Somerset. This was GEORGE VILLIERS, the youngest son of a Leicestershire gentleman: who came to Court with all the Paris fashions on him, and could dance as well as the best mountebank that ever was seen. He soon danced himself into the good graces of his Sowship, and danced the other favourite out of favour. Then, it was all at once discovered that the Earl and Countess of Somerset had not deserved all those great promotions and mighty rejoicings, and they were separately tried for the murder of Sir Thomas Overbury, and for other crimes. But, the King was so afraid of his late favourite's publicly telling some disgraceful things he knew of him—which he darkly threatened to do—that he was even examined with two men standing, one on either side of him, each with a cloak in his hand, ready to throw it over his head and stop his mouth if he should break out with what he had it in his power to tell. So, a very lame affair was purposely made of the trial, and his punishment was an allowance of four thousand pounds a year in retirement, while the Countess was pardoned, and allowed to pass into retirement too. They hated one another by this time, and lived to revile and torment each other some years.

While these events were in progress, and while his Sowship was making such an exhibition of himself, from day to day and from year to year, as is not often seen in any sty, three remarkable deaths took place in England. The first was that of the Minister, Robert Cecil, Earl of Salisbury, who was past sixty, and had never been strong, being deformed from his birth. He said at last that he had no wish to live; and no Minister need have had, with his experience of the meanness and wickedness of those disgraceful times. The second was that of the Lady Arabella Stuart, who alarmed his Sowship mightily, by privately marrying WILLIAM SEYMOUR, son of LORD BEAUCHAMP, who was a descendant of King Henry the Seventh, and who, his Sowship thought, might consequently increase and strengthen any claim she might one day set up to the throne. She was separated from her husband (who was put in the Tower) and thrust into a boat to be confined at Durham. She escaped in a man's dress to get away in a French ship from Gravesend to France, but unhappily missed her husband, who had escaped too, and was soon taken. She went raving mad in the miserable Tower, and died there after four years. The last, and the most important of these three deaths, was that of Prince Henry, the heir to the throne, in the nineteenth year of his age. He was a promising young prince, and greatly liked; a quiet, well-conducted youth, of whom two very good things are known: first, that his father was jealous of him; secondly, that he was the friend of Sir Walter Raleigh, languishing through all those years in the Tower, and often said that no man but his father would keep such a bird in such a cage. On the occasion of the preparations for the marriage of his sister the Princess Elizabeth with a foreign prince (and an unhappy marriage it turned out), he came from Richmond, where he had been very ill, to greet his new brother-in-law, at the palace at

Whitehall. There he played a great game at tennis, in his shirt, though it was very cold weather, and was seized with an alarming illness, and died within a fortnight of a putrid fever. For this young prince Sir Walter Raleigh wrote, in his prison in the Tower, the beginning of a History of the World: a wonderful instance how little his Sowship could do to confine a great man's mind, however long he might imprison his body.

And this mention of Sir Walter Raleigh, who had many faults, but who never showed so many merits as in trouble and adversity, may bring me at once to the end of his sad story. After an imprisonment in the Tower of twelve long years, he proposed to resume those old sea voyages of his, and to go to South America in search of gold. His Sowship, divided between his wish to be on good terms with the Spaniards through whose territory Sir Walter must pass (he had long had an idea of marrying Prince Henry to a Spanish Princess), and his avaricious eagerness to get hold of the gold, did not know what to do. But, in the end, he set Sir Walter free, taking securities for his return; and Sir Walter fitted out an expedition at his own cost and, on the twenty-eighth of March, one thousand six hundred and seventeen, sailed away in command of one of its ships, which he ominously called the Destiny. The expedition failed; the common men, not finding the gold they had expected, mutinied; a quarrel broke out between Sir Walter and the Spaniards, who hated him for old successes of his against them; and he took and burnt a little town called SAINT THOMAS. For this he was denounced to his Sowship by the Spanish Ambassador as a pirate; and returning almost broken-hearted, with his hopes and fortunes shattered, his company of friends dispersed, and his brave son (who had been one of them) killed, he was taken—through the treachery of SIR LEWIS STUKELY, his near relation, a scoundrel and a Vice-Admiral—and was once again immured in his prison-home of so many years.

His Sowship being mightily disappointed in not getting any gold, Sir Walter Raleigh was tried as unfairly, and with as many lies and evasions as the judges and law officers and every other authority in Church and State habitually practised under such a King. After a great deal of prevarication on all parts but his own, it was declared that he must die under his former sentence, now fifteen years old. So, on the twenty-eighth of October, one thousand six hundred and eighteen, he was shut up in the Gate House at Westminster to pass his last night on earth, and there he took leave of his good and faithful lady who was worthy to have lived in better days. At eight o'clock next morning, after a cheerful breakfast, and a pipe, and a cup of good wine, he was taken to Old Palace Yard in Westminster, where the scaffold was set up, and where so many people of high degree were assembled to see him die, that it was a matter of some difficulty to get him through the crowd. He behaved most nobly, but if anything lay heavy on his mind, it was that Earl of Essex, whose head he had seen roll off; and he solemnly said that he had had no hand in bringing him to the block, and that he had shed tears for him when he died. As the morning was very cold, the Sheriff said, would he come down to a fire for a little space, and warm himself? But Sir Walter thanked him, and said no, he would rather it were done at once, for he was ill of fever and ague, and in another quarter of an hour his shaking fit would come upon him if he were still alive, and his enemies might then suppose that he trembled for fear. With that, he kneeled and made a very beautiful and Christian prayer. Before he laid his head upon the block he felt the edge of the axe, and said, with a smile upon his face, that it was a sharp medicine, but would cure the worst disease. When he was bent down ready for death, he said to the executioner, finding that he hesitated, 'What dost thou fear? Strike, man!' So, the axe came down and struck his head off, in the sixty-sixth year of his age.

The new favourite got on fast. He was made a viscount, he was made Duke of Buckingham, he was made a marquis, he was made Master of the Horse, he was made Lord High Admiral—and the Chief Commander of the gallant English forces that had dispersed the Spanish Armada, was displaced to make room for him. He had the whole kingdom at his disposal, and his mother sold all the profits and honours of the State, as if she had kept a shop. He blazed all over with diamonds and other precious stones, from his hatband and his earrings to his shoes. Yet he was an ignorant presumptuous swaggering compound of knave and fool, with nothing but his beauty and his dancing to recommend him. This is the gentleman who called himself his Majesty's dog and slave, and called his Majesty Your Sowship. His Sowship called him STEENIE; it is supposed, because that was a nickname for Stephen, and because St Stephen was generally represented in pictures as a handsome saint.

His Sowship was driven sometimes to his wits'-end by his trimming between the general dislike of the Catholic religion at home, and his desire to wheedle and flatter it abroad, as his only means of getting a rich princess for his son's wife: a part of whose fortune he might cram into his greasy pockets. Prince Charles—or as his Sowship called him, Baby Charles—being now PRINCE OF WALES, the old project of a marriage with the Spanish King's daughter had been revived for him; and as she could not marry a Protestant without leave from the Pope, his Sowship himself secretly and meanly wrote to his Infallibility, asking for it. The negotiation for this Spanish marriage takes up a larger space in great books, than you can imagine, but the upshot of it all is, that when it had been held off by the Spanish Court for a long time, Baby Charles and Steenie set off in disguise as Mr Thomas Smith and Mr John Smith, to see the Spanish Princess; that Baby Charles pretended to be desperately in love with her, and jumped off walls to look at her, and made a considerable fool of himself in a good many ways; that she was called Princess of Wales and that the whole Spanish Court believed Baby Charles to be all but dying for her sake, as he expressly told them he was; that Baby Charles and Steenie came back to England, and were received with as much rapture as if they had been a blessing to it; that Baby Charles had actually fallen in love with HENRIETTA MARIA, the French King's sister, whom he had seen in Paris; that he thought it a wonderfully fine and princely thing to have deceived the Spaniards, all through; and that he openly said, with a chuckle, as soon as he was safe and sound at home again, that the Spaniards were great fools to have believed him.

Like most dishonest men, the Prince and the favourite complained that the people whom they had deluded were dishonest. They made such misrepresentations of the treachery of the Spaniards in this business of the Spanish match, that the English nation became eager for a war with them. Although the gravest Spaniards laughed at the idea of his Sowship in a warlike attitude, the Parliament granted money for the beginning of hostilities, and the treaties with Spain were publicly declared to be at an end. The Spanish ambassador in London —probably with the help of the fallen favourite, the Earl of Somerset—being unable to obtain speech with his Sowship, slipped a paper into his hand, declaring that he was a prisoner in his own house, and was entirely governed by Buckingham and his creatures. The first effect of this letter was that his Sowship began to cry and whine, and took Baby Charles away from Steenie, and went down to Windsor, gabbling all sorts of nonsense. The end of it was that his Sowship hugged his dog and slave, and said he was quite satisfied.

He had given the Prince and the favourite almost unlimited power to settle anything with the Pope as to the Spanish marriage; and he now, with a view to the French one, signed a treaty that all Roman Catholics in England should exercise their religion freely, and should never be required to take any oath contrary thereto. In return for this, and for other concessions much less to be defended, Henrietta Maria was to become the Prince's wife, and was to bring him a fortune of eight hundred thousand crowns.

His Sowship's eyes were getting red with

eagerly looking for the money, when the end of a gluttonous life came upon him; and, after a fortnight's illness, on Sunday the twenty-seventh of March, one thousand six hundred and twenty-five, he died. He had reigned twenty-two years, and was fifty-nine years old. I know of nothing more abominable in history than the adulation that was lavished on this King, and the vice and corruption that such a barefaced habit of lying produced in his court. It is much to be doubted whether one man of honour, and not utterly self-disgraced, kept his place near James the First. Lord Bacon, that able and wise philosopher, as the First Judge in the Kingdom in this reign, became a public spectacle of dishonesty and corruption; and in his base flattery of his Sowship, and in his crawling servility to his dog and slave, disgraced himself even more. But, a creature like his Sowship set upon a throne is like the Plague, and everybody receives infection from him.

England under Charles the First

Baby Charles became KING CHARLES THE FIRST, in the twenty-fifth year of his age. Unlike his father, he was usually amiable in his private character, and grave and dignified in his bearing; but, like his father, he had monstrously exaggerated notions of the rights of a king, and was evasive, and not to be trusted. If his word could have been relied upon, his history might have had a different end.

His first care was to send over that insolent upstart, Buckingham, to bring Henrietta Maria from Paris to be his Queen; upon which occasion Buckingham—with his usual audacity—made love to the young Queen of Austria, and was very indignant indeed with CARDINAL RICHELIEU, the French Minister, for thwarting his intentions. The English people were very well disposed to like their new Queen, and to receive her with great favour when she came among them as a stranger. But, she held the Protestant religion in great dislike, and brought over a crowd of unpleasant priests, who made her do some very ridiculous things, and forced themselves upon the public notice in many disagreeable ways. Hence, the people soon came to dislike her, and she soon came to dislike them; and she did so much all through this reign in setting the King (who was dotingly fond of her) against his subjects, that it would have been better for him if she had never been born.

Now, you are to understand that King Charles the First—of his own determination to be a high and mighty King not to be called to account by anybody, and urged on by his Queen besides—deliberately set himself to put his Parliament down and to put himself up. You are also to understand, that even in pursuit of this wrong idea (enough in itself to have ruined any king) he never took a straight course, but always took a crooked one.

He was bent upon war with Spain, though neither the House of Commons nor the people were quite clear as to the justice of that war, now that they began to think a little more about the story of the Spanish match. But the King rushed into it hotly, raised money by illegal means to meet its expenses, and encountered a miserable failure at Cadiz, in the very first year of his reign. An expedition to Cadiz had been made in the hope of plunder, but as it was not successful, it was necessary to get a grant of money from the Parliament; and when they met, in no very complying humour, the King told them, 'to make haste to let him have it, or it would be the worse for themselves.' Not put in a more complying humour by this, they impeached the King's favourite, the Duke of

Buckingham, as the cause (which he undoubtedly was) of many great public grievances and wrongs. The King, to save him, dissolved the Parliament without getting the money he wanted; and when the Lords implored him to consider and grant a little delay, he replied, 'No, not one minute.' He then began to raise money for himself by the following means among others.

He levied certain duties called tonnage and poundage which had not been granted by the Parliament, and could lawfully be levied by no other power; he called upon the seaport towns to furnish, and to pay all the cost for three months of, a fleet of armed ships; and he required the people to unite in lending him large sums of money, the repayment of which was very doubtful. If the poor people refused, they were pressed as soldiers or sailors; if the gentry refused, they were sent to prison. Five gentlemen, named SIR THOMAS DARNEL, JOHN CORBET, WALTER EARL, JOHN HEVENINGHAM, and EVERARD HAMPDEN, for refusing were taken up by a warrant of the King's privy council, and were sent to prison without any cause but the King's pleasure being stated for their imprisonment. Then the question came to be solemnly tried, whether this was not a violation of Magna Charta, and an encroachment by the King on the highest rights of the English people. His lawyers contended No, because to encroach upon the rights of the English people would be to do wrong, and the King could do no wrong. The accommodating judges decided in favour of this wicked nonsense; and here was a fatal division between the King and the people.

For all this, it became necessary to call another Parliament. The people, sensible of the danger in which their liberties were, chose for it those who were best known for their determined opposition to the King; but still the King, quite blinded by his determination to carry everything before him, addressed them when they met, in a contemptuous manner, and just told them in so many words that he had only called them together because he wanted money. The Parliament, strong enough and resolute enough to know that they would lower his tone, cared little for what he said, and laid before him one of the great documents of history, which is called the PETITION OF RIGHT, requiring that the free men of England should no longer be called upon to lend the King money, and should no longer be pressed or imprisoned for refusing to do so; further, that the free men of England should no longer be seized by the King's special mandate or warrant, it being contrary to their rights and liberties and the laws of their country. At first the King returned an answer to this petition, in which he tried to shirk it altogether; but, the House of Commons then showing their determination to go on with the impeachment of Buckingham, the King in alarm returned an answer, giving his consent to all that was required of him. He not only afterwards departed from his word and honour on these points, over and over again, but, at this very time, he did the mean and dissembling act of publishing his first answer and not his second—merely that the people might suppose that the Parliament had not got the better of him.

That pestilent Buckingham, to gratify his own wounded vanity, had by this time involved the country in war with France, as well as with Spain. For such miserable causes and such miserable creatures are wars sometimes made! But he was destined to do little more mischief in this world.

One morning, as he was going out of his house to his carriage, he turned to speak to a certain Colonel FRYER who was with him; and he was violently stabbed with a knife, which the murderer left sticking in his heart. This happened in his hall. He had had angry words up-stairs, just before, with some French gentlemen, who were immediately suspected by his servants, and had a close escape from being set upon and killed. In the midst of the noise, the real murderer, who had gone to the kitchen and might easily have got away, drew his sword and cried out, 'I am the man!' His name was JOHN FELTON, a Protestant and a retired officer in the army. He said he had had no personal ill-will to the Duke, but had killed him as a curse to the country. He had aimed his blow well, for Buckingham had only had time to cry out, 'Villain!' and then he drew out the knife, fell against a table, and died.

The council made a mighty business of examining John Felton about this murder, though it was a plain case enough, one would think. He had come seventy miles to do it, he told them, and he did it for the reason he had declared; if they put him upon the rack, as that noble MARQUIS OF

DORSET whom he saw before him, had the goodness to threaten, he gave that marquis warning, that he would accuse *him* as his accomplice! The King was unpleasantly anxious to have him racked, nevertheless; but as the judges now found out that torture was contrary to the law of England—it is a pity they did not make the discovery a little sooner—John Felton was simply executed for the murder he had done. A murder it undoubtedly was, and not in the least to be defended: though he had freed England from one of the most profligate, contemptible, and base court favourites to whom it has ever yielded.

A very different man now arose. This was SIR THOMAS WENTWORTH, a Yorkshire gentleman, who had sat in Parliament for a long time, and who had favoured arbitrary and haughty principles, but who had gone over to the people's side on receiving offence from Buckingham. The King, much wanting such a man—for, besides being naturally favourable to the King's cause, he had great abilities—made him first a Baron, and then a Viscount, and gave him high employment, and won him most completely.

A Parliament, however, was still in existence,

and was *not* to be won. On the twentieth of January, one thousand six hundred and twenty-nine, SIR JOHN ELIOT, a great man who had been active in the Petition of Right, brought forward other strong resolutions against the King's chief instruments, and called upon the Speaker to put them to the vote. To this the Speaker answered, 'he was commanded otherwise by the King,' and got up to leave the chair—which, according to the rules of the House of Commons would have obliged it to adjourn without doing anything more—when two members, named MR HOLLIS and MR VALENTINE, held him down. A scene of great confusion arose among the members; and while many swords were drawn and flashing about, the King, who was kept informed of all that was going on, told the captain of his guard to go down to the House and force the doors. The resolutions were by that time, however, voted, and the House adjourned. Sir John Eliot and those two members who had held the Speaker down, were quickly summoned before the council. As they claimed it to be their privilege not to answer out of Parliament for anything they had said in it, they were committed to the Tower. The King then went down and dissolved the Parliament, in a speech wherein he made mention of these gentlemen as 'Vipers'—which did not do him much good that ever I have heard of.

As they refused to gain their liberty by saying they were sorry for what they had done, the King, always remarkably unforgiving, never overlooked their offence. When they demanded to be brought up before the court of King's Bench, he even resorted to the meanness of having them moved about from prison to prison, so that the writs issued for that purpose should not legally find them. At last they came before the court and were sentenced to heavy fines, and to be imprisoned during the King's pleasure. When Sir John Eliot's health had quite given way, and he so longed for change of air and scene as to petition for his release, the King sent back the answer (worthy of his Sowship himself) that the petition was not humble enough. When he sent another petition by his young son, in which he pathetically offered to go back to prison when his health was restored, if he might be released for its recovery, the King still disregarded it. When he died in the Tower, and his children petitioned to be allowed to take his body down to Cornwall, there to lay it among the ashes of his forefathers, the King returned for answer, 'Let Sir John Eliot's body be buried in the church of that parish where he died.' All this was like a very little King indeed, I think.

And now, for twelve long years, steadily pursuing his design of setting himself up and putting the people down, the King called no Parliament; but ruled without one. If twelve thousand volumes were written in his praise (as a good many have been) it would still remain a fact, impossible to be denied, that for twelve years King Charles the First reigned in England unlawfully and despotically, seized upon his subjects' goods and money at his pleasure, and punished according to his unbridled will all who ventured to oppose him. It is a fashion with some people to think that this King's career was cut short; but I must say myself that I think he ran a pretty long one.

WILLIAM LAUD, Archbishop of Canterbury, was the King's right-hand man in the religious part of the putting down of the people's liberties. Laud, who was a sincere man, of large learning but small sense—for the two things sometimes go together in very different quantities—though a

Protestant, held opinions so near those of the Catholics, that the Pope wanted to make a Cardinal of him, if he would have accepted that favour. He looked upon vows, robes, lighted candles, images, and so forth, as amazingly important in religious ceremonies; and he brought in an immensity of bowing and candle-snuffing. He also regarded archbishops and bishops as a sort of miraculous persons, and was inveterate in the last degree against any who thought otherwise. Accordingly, he offered up thanks to Heaven, and was in a state of much pious pleasure, when a Scotch clergyman, named LEIGHTON, was pilloried, whipped, branded in the cheek, and had one of his ears cut off and one of his nostrils slit, for calling bishops trumpery and the inventions of men. He originated on a Sunday morning the prosecution of WILLIAM PRYNNE, a barrister who was of similar opinions, and who was fined a thousand pounds; who was pilloried; who had his ears cut off on two occasions—one ear at a time—and who was imprisoned for life. He highly approved of the punishment of DOCTOR BASTWICK, a physician; who was also fined a thousand pounds; and who afterwards had *his* ears cut off, and was imprisoned for life. These were gentle methods of persuasion, some will tell you: I think, they were rather calculated to be alarming to the people.

In the money part of the putting down of the people's liberties, the King was equally gentle, as some will tell you: as I think, equally alarming. He levied those duties of tonnage and poundage, and increased them as he thought fit. He granted monopolies to companies of merchants on their paying him for them, notwithstanding the great complaints that had, for years and years, been made on the subject of monopolies. He fined the people for disobeying proclamations issued by his Sowship in direct violation of law. He revived the detested Forest laws, and took private property to himself as his forest right. Above all, he determined to have what was called Ship Money; that is to say, money for the support of the fleet—not only from the seaports, but from all the counties of England: having found out that, in some ancient time or other, all the counties paid it. The grievance of this ship money being somewhat too strong, JOHN CHAMBERS, a citizen of London, refused to pay his part of it. For this the Lord Mayor ordered John Chambers to prison, and for that John Chambers brought a suit against the Lord Mayor. LORD SAY, also, behaved like a real nobleman, and declared he would not pay. But, the sturdiest and best opponent of the ship money was JOHN HAMPDEN, a gentleman of Buckinghamshire, who had sat among the 'vipers' in the House of Commons when there was such a thing, and who had been the bosom friend of Sir John Eliot. This case was tried before the twelve judges in the Court of Exchequer, and again the King's lawyers said it was impossible that ship money could be wrong, because the King could do no wrong, however hard he tried—and he really did try very hard during these twelve years. Seven of the judges said that was quite true, and Mr Hampden was bound to pay: five of the judges said that was quite false, and Mr Hampden was not bound to pay. So, the King triumphed (as he thought), by making Hampden the most popular man in England; where matters were getting to that height now, that many honest Englishmen could not endure their country, and sailed away across the seas to found a colony in Massachusetts Bay in America. It is said that Hampden himself and his relation OLIVER CROMWELL were going with a company of such voyagers, and were actually on board ship, when they were stopped by a proclamation, prohibiting sea captains to carry out such passengers without the royal license. But O! it would have been well for the King if he had let them go!

This was the state of England. If Laud had been a madman just broke loose, he could not have done more mischief than he did in Scotland. In his endeavours (in which he was seconded by the King, then in person in that part of his dominions) to force his own ideas of bishops, and his own religious forms and ceremonies upon the Scotch, he roused that nation to a perfect frenzy. They formed a solemn league, which they called The Covenant, for the preservation of their own religious forms; they rose in arms throughout the whole country; they summoned all their men to prayers and sermons twice a day by beat of drum; they sang psalms, in which they compared their enemies to all the evil spirits that ever were heard of; and they solemnly vowed to smite them with the sword. At first the King tried force, then treaty, then a Scottish Parliament which did not answer at all. Then he tried the EARL OF STRAFFORD, formerly Sir Thomas Wentworth; who, as LORD WENTWORTH, had been governing Ireland. He, too, had carried it with a very high hand there, though to the benefit and prosperity of that country.

Strafford and Laud were for conquering the Scottish people by force of arms. Other lords who were taken into council, recommended that a Parliament should at last be called; to which the King unwillingly consented. So, on the thirteenth of April, one thousand six hundred and forty, that then strange sight, a Parliament, was seen at Westminster. It is called the Short Parliament, for it lasted a very little while. While the members were all looking at one another, doubtful who would dare to speak, MR PYM arose and set forth all that the King had done unlawfully during the past twelve years, and what was the position to which England was reduced. This great example set, other members took courage and spoke the truth freely, though with great patience and moderation. The King, a little frightened, sent to say that if they would grant him a certain sum on certain terms, no more ship money should be raised. They debated the matter for two days; and then, as they would not give him all he asked without promise or inquiry, he dissolved them.

But they knew very well that he must have a Parliament now; and he began to make that discovery too, though rather late in the day. Wherefore, on the twenty-fourth of September, being then at York with an army collected against the Scottish people, but his own men sullen and discontented like the rest of the nation, the King told the great council of the Lords, whom he had called to meet him there, that he would summon another Parliament to assemble on the third of November. The soldiers of the Covenant had now forced their way into England and had taken possession of the northern counties, where the coals are got. As it would never do to be without coals, and as the King's troops could make no head against the Covenanters so full of gloomy zeal, a truce was made, and a treaty with Scotland was taken into consideration. Meanwhile the northern counties paid the Covenanters to leave the coals alone, and keep quiet.

We have now disposed of the Short Parliament. We have next to see what memorable things were done by the Long one.

The Long Parliament assembled on the third of November, one thousand six hundred and forty-one. That day week the Earl of Strafford arrived from York, very sensible that the spirited and determined men who formed that Parliament were no friends towards him, who had not only deserted the cause of the people, but who had on all occasions opposed himself to their liberties. The King told him, for his comfort, that the Parliament 'should not hurt one hair of his head.' But, on the very next day Mr Pym, in the House of Commons, and with great solemnity, impeached the Earl of Strafford as a traitor. He was immediately taken into custody and fell from his proud height.

It was the twenty-second of March before he was brought to trial in Westminster Hall; where, although he was very ill and suffered great pain, he defended himself with such ability and majesty, that it was doubtful whether he would not get the best of it. But on the thirteenth day of the trial, Pym produced in the House of Commons a copy of some notes of a council, found by young SIR HARRY VANE in a red velvet cabinet belonging to his father (Secretary Vane, who sat at the council-table with the Earl), in which Strafford had distinctly told the King that he was free from all rules and obligations of government, and might do with his people whatever he liked; and in which he had added—'You have an army in Ireland that you may employ to reduce this kingdom to obedience.' It was not clear whether by the words 'this kingdom,' he had really meant England or Scotland; but the Parliament contended that he meant England, and this was treason. At the same sitting of the House of Commons it was resolved to bring in a bill of attainder declaring the treason to have been committed: in preference to proceeding with the trial by impeachment, which would have required the treason to be proved.

So, a bill was brought in at once, was carried through the House of Commons by a large majority, and was sent up to the House of Lords. While it was still uncertain whether the House of Lords would pass it and the King consent to it, Pym disclosed to the House of Commons that the King and Queen had both been plotting with the officers of the army to bring up the soldiers and control the Parliament, and also to introduce two hundred soldiers into the Tower of London to effect the Earl's escape. The plotting with the army was revealed by one GEORGE GORING, the son of a lord of that name: a bad fellow who was one of the original plotters, and turned traitor. The King had actually given his warrant for the admission of the two hundred men into the Tower, and they would have got in too, but for the refusal of the governor—a sturdy Scotchman of the name of BALFOUR—to admit them. These matters being made public, great numbers of people began to riot outside the Houses of Parliament, and to cry out for the execution of the Earl of Strafford, as one of the King's chief instruments against them. The bill passed the House of Lords while the people were in this state of agitation, and was laid before the King for his assent, together with another bill declaring that the Parliament then assembled should not be dissolved or adjourned without their own consent. The King—not unwilling to save a faithful servant, though he had no great attachment for him—was in some doubt what to do; but he gave his consent to both bills, although he in his heart believed that the bill against the Earl of Strafford was unlawful and unjust. The Earl had written to him, telling him that he was willing to die for his sake. But he had not expected that his royal master would take him at his word quite so readily; for, when he heard his doom, he laid his hand upon his heart, and said, 'Put not your trust in Princes!'

The King, who never could be straightforward and plain, through one single day or through one single sheet of paper, wrote a letter to the Lords, and sent it by the young Prince of Wales, entreating them to prevail with the Commons that 'that unfortunate man should fulfil the natural course of his life in a close imprisonment.' In a postscript to the very same letter, he added, 'If he must die, it were charity to reprieve him till Saturday.' If there had been any doubt of his fate, this weakness and meanness would have settled it. The very next day, which was the twelfth of May, he was brought out to be beheaded on Tower Hill.

Archbishop Laud, who had been so fond of having people's ears cropped off and their noses slit, was now confined in the Tower too; and when the Earl went by his window to his death, he was there, at his request, to give him his blessing. They had been great friends in the King's cause, and the Earl had written to him in the days of their power that he thought it would be an admirable thing to have Mr Hampden publicly whipped for refusing to pay the ship money. However, those high and mighty doings were over now, and the Earl went his way to death with dignity and heroism. The governor wished him to get into a coach at the Tower gate, for fear the people should tear him to pieces; but he said it was all one to him whether he died by the axe or by the people's hands. So, he walked, with a firm tread and a stately look, and sometimes pulled off his hat to them as he passed along. They were profoundly quiet. He made a speech on the scaffold from some notes he had prepared (the paper was found lying there after his head was struck off), and one blow of the axe killed him, in the forty-ninth year of his age.

This bold and daring act, the Parliament accompanied by other famous measures, all originating (as even this did) in the King's having so grossly and so long abused his power. The name of DELINQUENTS was applied to all sheriffs and other officers who had been concerned in raising the ship money, or any other money, from the people, in an unlawful manner; the Hampden judgment was reversed; the judges who had decided against Hampden were called upon to give large securities that they would take such consequences as Parliament might impose upon them; and one was arrested as he sat in High Court, and carried off to prison. Laud was impeached; the unfortunate victims whose ears had been cropped and whose noses had been slit, were brought out of prison in triumph; and a bill was passed declaring that a Parliament should be called every third year, and that if the King and the King's officers did not call it, the people should assemble of themselves and summon it, as of their own right and power. Great illuminations and rejoicings took place over all these things, and the country was wildly excited. That the Parliament took advantage of this excitement and stirred them up by every means, there is no doubt; but you are always to remember those twelve long years, during which the King had tried so hard whether he really could do any wrong or not.

All this time there was a great religious outcry against the right of the Bishops to sit in Parliament; to which the Scottish people particularly objected. The English were divided on this subject, and, partly on this account and partly because they had had foolish expectations that the

Parliament would be able to take off nearly all the taxes, numbers of them sometimes wavered and inclined towards the King.

I believe myself, that if, at this or almost any other period of his life, the King could have been trusted by any man not out of his senses, he might have saved himself and kept his throne. But, on the English army being disbanded, he plotted with the officers again, as he had done before, and established the fact beyond all doubt by putting his signature of approval to a petition against the Parliamentary leaders, which was drawn up by certain officers. When the Scottish army was disbanded, he went to Edinburgh in four days—which was going very fast at that time—to plot again, and so darkly too, that it is difficult to decide what his whole object was. Some suppose that he wanted to gain over the Scottish Parliament, as he did in fact gain over, by presents and favours, many Scottish lords and men of power. Some think that he went to get proofs against the Parliamentary leaders in England of their having treasonably invited the Scottish people to come and help them. With whatever object he went to Scotland, he did little good by going. At the instigation of the EARL OF MONTROSE, a desperate man who was then in prison for plotting, he tried to kidnap three Scottish lords who escaped. A committee of the Parliament at home, who had followed to watch him, writing an account of this INCIDENT, as it was called, to the Parliament, the Parliament made a fresh stir about it; were, or feigned to be, much alarmed for themselves; and wrote to the EARL OF ESSEX, the commander-in-chief, for a guard to protect them.

It is not absolutely proved that the King plotted in Ireland besides, but it is very probable that he did, and that the Queen did, and that he had some wild hope of gaining the Irish people over to his side by favouring a rise among them. Whether or no, they did rise in a most brutal and savage rebellion; in which, encouraged by their priests, they committed such atrocities upon numbers of the English, of both sexes and of all ages, as nobody could believe, but for their being related on oath by eye-witnesses. Whether one hundred thousand or two hundred thousand Protestants were murdered in this outbreak, is uncertain; but, that it was as ruthless and barbarous an outbreak as ever was known among any savage people, is certain.

The King came home from Scotland, determined to make a great struggle for his lost power. He believed that, through his presents and favours, Scotland would take no part against him; and the Lord Mayor of London received him with such a magnificent dinner that he thought he must have become popular again in England. It would take a good many Lord Mayors, however, to make a people, and the King soon found himself mistaken.

Not so soon, though, but that there was a great opposition in the Parliament to a celebrated paper put forth by Pym and Hampden and the rest, called 'THE REMONSTRANCE,' which set forth all the illegal acts that the King had ever done, but politely laid the blame of them on his bad advisers. Even when it was passed and presented to him, the King still thought himself strong enough to discharge Balfour from his command in the Tower, and to put in his place a man of bad character; to whom the Commons instantly objected, and whom he was obliged to abandon. At this time, the old outcry about the Bishops became louder than ever, and the old Archbishop of York was so near being murdered as he went down to the House of Lords—being laid hold of by the mob and violently knocked about, in return for very foolishly scolding a shrill boy who was yelping out 'No Bishops!'—that he sent for all the Bishops who were in town, and proposed to them to sign a declaration that, as they could no longer without danger to their lives attend their duty in Parliament, they protested against the lawfulness of everything done in their absence. This they asked the King to send to the House of Lords, which he did. Then the House of Commons impeached the whole party of Bishops and sent them off to the Tower.

Taking no warning from this; but encouraged by there being a moderate party in the Parliament who objected to these strong measures, the King, on the third of January, one thousand six hundred and forty-two, took the rashest step that ever was taken by mortal man.

Of his own accord and without advice, he sent the Attorney-General to the House of Lords, to accuse of treason certain members of Parliament who as popular leaders were the most obnoxious to him: LORD KIMBOLTON, SIR ARTHUR HASELRIG, DENZIL HOLLIS, JOHN PYM (they used to call him King Pym, he possessed such power and looked so big), JOHN HAMPDEN, and WILLIAM STRODE. The houses of those members he caused to be entered, and their papers to be sealed up. At the same time, he sent a messenger to the House of Commons demanding to have the five gentlemen who were members of that House immediately produced. To this the House replied that they should appear as soon as there was any legal charge against them, and immediately adjourned.

Next day, the House of Commons send into the City to let the Lord Mayor know that their privileges are invaded by the King, and that there is no safety for anybody or anything. Then, when the five members are gone out of the way, down comes the King himself, with all his guard and from two to three hundred gentlemen and soldiers, of whom the greater part were armed. These he leaves in the hall; and then, with his nephew at his side, goes into the House, takes off his hat, and walks up to the Speaker's chair. The Speaker leaves it, the King stands in front of it, looks about him steadily for a little while, and says he has come for those five members. No one speaks, and then he calls John Pym by name. No one speaks, and then he calls Denzil Hollis by name. No one speaks, and then he asks the Speaker of the House where those five members are? The Speaker, answering on his knee, nobly replies that he is the servant of that House, and that he has neither eyes to see, nor tongue to speak, anything but what the House commands him. Upon this, the King, beaten from that time evermore, replies that he will seek them himself, for they have committed treason; and goes out, with his hat in his hand, amid some audible murmurs from the members.

No words can describe the hurry that arose out of doors when all this was known. The five members had gone for safety to a house in Coleman-street, in the City, where they were guarded all night; and indeed the whole city watched in arms like an army. At ten o'clock in the morning, the King, already frightened at what he had done, came to the Guildhall, with only half a dozen lords, and made a speech to the people, hoping they would not shelter those whom he accused of treason. Next day, he issued a proclamation for the apprehension of the five members; but the Parliament minded it so little that they made great arrangements for having them brought down to

Westminster in great state, five days afterwards. The King was so alarmed now at his own imprudence, if not for his own safety, that he left his palace at Whitehall, and went away with his Queen and children to Hampton Court.

It was the eleventh of May, when the five members were carried in state and triumph to Westminster. They were taken by water. The river could not be seen for the boats on it; and the five members were hemmed in by barges full of men and great guns, ready to protect them, at any cost. Along the Strand a large body of the train-bands of London, under their commander, SKIPPON, marched to be ready to assist the little fleet. Beyond them, came a crowd who choked the streets, roaring incessantly about the Bishops and the Papists, and crying out contemptuously as they passed Whitehall, 'What has become of the King?' With this great noise outside the House of Commons, and with great silence within, Mr Pym rose and informed the House of the great kindness with which they had been received in the City. Upon that, the House called the sheriffs in and thanked them, and requested the train-bands, under their commander Skippon, to guard the

House of Commons every day. Then, came four thousand men on horseback out of Buckinghamshire, offering their services as a guard too, and bearing a petition to the King, complaining of the injury that had been done to Mr Hampden, who was their county man and much beloved and honoured.

When the King set off for Hampton Court, the gentlemen and soldiers who had been with him followed him out of town as far as Kingston-upon-Thames; next day, Lord Digby came to them from the King at Hampton Court, in his coach and six, to inform them that the King accepted their protection. This, the Parliament said, was making war against the kingdom, and Lord Digby fled abroad. The Parliament then immediately applied themselves to getting hold of the military power of the country, well knowing that the King was already trying hard to use it against them, and that he had secretly sent the Earl of Newcastle to Hull, to secure a valuable magazine of arms and gunpowder that was there. In those times, every county had its own magazines of arms and powder, for its own train-bands or militia; so, the Parliament brought in a bill claiming the right (which up to this time had belonged to the King) of appointing the Lord Lieutenants of counties, who commanded these train-bands; also, of having all the forts, castles, and garrisons in the kingdom, put into the hands of such governors as they, the Parliament, could confide in. It also passed a law depriving the Bishops of their votes. The King gave his assent to that bill, but would not abandon the right of appointing the Lord Lieutenants, though he said he was willing to appoint such as might be suggested to him by the Parliament. When the Earl of Pembroke asked him whether he would not give way on that question for a time, he said, 'By God! not for one hour!' and upon this he and the Parliament went to war.

His young daughter was betrothed to the Prince of Orange. On pretence of taking her to the country of her future husband, the Queen was already got safely away to Holland, there to pawn the Crown jewels for money to raise an army on the King's side. The Lord Admiral being sick, the House of Commons now named the Earl of Warwick to hold his place for a year. The King named another gentleman; the House of Commons took its own way, and the Earl of Warwick became

Lord Admiral without the King's consent. The Parliament sent orders down to Hull to have that magazine removed to London; the King went down to Hull to take it himself. The citizens would not admit him into the town, and the governor would not admit him into the castle. The Parliament resolved that whatever the two Houses passed, and the King would not consent to, should be called an ORDINANCE, and should be as much a law as if he did consent to it. The King protested against this, and gave notice that these ordinances were not to be obeyed. The King, attended by the majority of the House of Peers, and by many members of the House of Commons, established himself at York. The Chancellor went to him with the Great Seal, and the Parliament made a new Great Seal. The Queen sent over a ship full of arms and ammunition, and the King issued letters to borrow money at high interest. The Parliament raised twenty regiments of foot and seventy-five troops of horse; and the people willingly aided them with their money, plate, jewellery, and trinkets—the married women even with their wedding-rings. Every member of Parliament who could raise a troop or a regiment in his own part of the country, dressed it according to his taste and in his own colours, and commanded it. Foremost among them all, OLIVER CROMWELL raised a troop of horse—thoroughly in earnest and thoroughly well armed—who were, perhaps, the best soldiers that ever were seen.

In some of their proceedings, this famous Parliament passed the bounds of previous law and custom, yielded to and favoured riotous assemblages of the people, and acted tyrannically in imprisoning some who differed from the popular leaders. But again, you are always to remember that the twelve years during which the King had had his own wilful way, had gone before; and that nothing could make the times what they might, could, would, or should have been, if those twelve years had never rolled away.

I shall not try to relate the particulars of the great civil war between King Charles the First and the Long Parliament, which lasted nearly four years, and a full account of which would fill many large books. It was a sad thing that Englishmen should once more be fighting against Englishmen on English ground; but, it is some consolation to know that on both sides there was great humanity, forbearance, and honour. The soldiers of the Parliament were far more remarkable for these good qualities than the soldiers of the King (many of whom fought for mere pay without much caring for the cause); but those of the nobility and gentry who were on the King's side were so brave, and so faithful to him, that their conduct cannot but command our highest admiration. Among them were great numbers of Catholics, who took the royal side because the Queen was so strongly of their persuasion.

The King might have distinguished some of these gallant spirits, if he had been as generous a spirit himself, by giving them the command of his army. Instead of that, however, true to his old high notions of royalty, he entrusted it to his two nephews, PRINCE RUPERT and PRINCE MAURICE, who were of royal blood and came over from abroad to help him. It might have been better for him if they had stayed away; since Prince Rupert was an impetuous, hot-headed fellow, whose only idea was to dash into battle at all times and seasons, and lay about him.

The general-in-chief of the Parliamentary army was the Earl of Essex, a gentleman of honour and an excellent soldier. A little while before the war broke out, there had been some rioting at Westminster between certain officious law students and noisy soldiers, and the shopkeepers and their apprentices, and the general people in the streets. At that time the King's friends called the crowd, Roundheads, because the apprentices wore short hair; the crowd, in return, called their opponents Cavaliers, meaning that they were a blustering set, who pretended to be very military. These two words now began to be used to distinguish the two sides in the civil war. The Royalists also called the Parliamentary men Rebels and Rogues, while the Parliamentary men called *them* Malignants, and spoke of themselves as the Godly, the Honest, and so forth.

The war broke out at Portsmouth, where that double traitor Goring had again gone over to the King and was besieged by the Parliamentary troops. Upon this, the King proclaimed the Earl of Essex and the officers serving under him, traitors, and called upon his loyal subjects to meet him in arms at Nottingham on the twenty-fifth of August. But his loyal subjects came about him in scanty numbers, and it was a windy, gloomy day, and the

Royal Standard got blown down, and the whole affair was very melancholy. The chief engagements after this, took place in the vale of the Red Horse near Banbury, at Brentford, at Devizes, at Chalgrave Field (where Mr Hampden was so sorely wounded while fighting at the head of his men, that he died within a week), at Newbury (in which battle LORD FALKLAND, one of the best noblemen on the King's side, was killed), at Leicester, at Naseby, at Winchester, at Marston Moor near York, at Newcastle, and in many other parts of England and Scotland. These battles were attended with various successes. At one time, the King was victorious; at another time, the Parliament. But almost all the great and busy towns were against the King; and when it was considered necessary to fortify London, all ranks of people, from labouring men and women, up to lords and ladies, worked hard together with heartiness and good will. The most distinguished leaders on the Parliamentary side were HAMPDEN, SIR THOMAS FAIRFAX, and, above all, OLIVER CROMWELL, and his son-in-law IRETON.

During the whole of this war, the people, to whom it was very expensive and irksome, and to whom it was made the more distressing by almost every family being divided—some of its members attaching themselves to one side and some to the other—were over and over again most anxious for peace. So were some of the best men in each cause. Accordingly, treaties of peace were discussed between commissioners from the Parliament and the King; at York, at Oxford (where the King held a little Parliament of his own), and at Uxbridge. But they came to nothing. In all these negotiations, and in all his difficulties, the King showed himself at his best. He was courageous, cool, self-possessed, and clever; but, the old taint of his character was always in him, and he was never for one single moment to be trusted. Lord Clarendon, the historian, one of his highest admirers, supposes that he had unhappily promised the Queen never to make peace without her consent, and that this must often be taken as his excuse. He never kept his word from night to morning. He signed a cessation of hostilities with the blood-stained Irish rebels for a sum of money, and invited the Irish regiments over, to help him against the Parliament. In the battle of Naseby, his cabinet was seized and was found to contain a correspondence with the Queen, in which he expressly told her that he had deceived the Parliament—a mongrel Parliament, he called it now, as an improvement on his old term of vipers—in pretending to recognise it and to treat with it; and from which it further appeared that he had long been in secret treaty with the Duke of Lorraine for a foreign army of ten thousand men. Disappointed in this, he sent a most devoted friend of his, the EARL OF GLAMORGAN, to Ireland, to conclude a secret treaty with the Catholic powers, to send him an Irish army of ten thousand men; in return for which he was to bestow great favours on the Catholic religion. And, when this treaty was discovered in the carriage of a fighting Irish Archbishop who was killed in one of the many skirmishes of those days, he basely denied and deserted his attached friend, the Earl, on his being charged with high treason; and—even worse than this—had left blanks in the secret instructions he gave him with his own kingly hand, expressly that he might thus save himself.

At last, on the twenty-seventh day of April, one thousand six hundred and forty-six, the King found himself in the city of Oxford, so surrounded by the Parliamentary army who were closing in upon him on all sides that he felt that if he would escape he must delay no longer. So, that night, having altered the cut of his hair and beard, he was dressed up as a servant and put upon a horse with a cloak strapped behind him, and rode out of the town behind one of his own faithful followers, with a clergyman of that country who knew the road well, for a guide. He rode towards London as far as Harrow, and then altered his plans and resolved, it would seem, to go to the Scottish camp. The Scottish men had been invited over to help the Parliamentary army, and had a large force then in England. The King was so desperately intriguing in everything he did, that it is doubtful what he exactly meant by this step. He took it, anyhow, and delivered himself up to the EARL OF LEVEN, the Scottish general-in-chief, who treated him as an honourable prisoner. Negotiations between the Parliament on the one hand and the Scottish authorities on the other, as to what should be done with him, lasted until the following February. Then, when the King had refused to the Parliament the concession of that old militia point for twenty years, and had refused to Scotland the recognition of its Solemn League and Covenant, Scotland got a handsome sum for its army and its help, and the King into the bargain. He was taken, by certain Parliamentary commissioners appointed to receive him, to one of his own houses, called Holmby House, near Althorpe, in Northamptonshire.

While the Civil War was still in progress, John Pym died, and was buried with great honour in Westminster Abbey—not with greater honour than he deserved, for the liberties of Englishmen owe a mighty debt to Pym and Hampden. The war was but newly over when the Earl of Essex died, of an illness brought on by his having overheated himself in a stag hunt in Windsor Forest. He, too, was buried in Westminster Abbey, with great state. I wish it were not necessary to add that Archbishop Laud died upon the scaffold when the war was not yet done. His trial lasted in all nearly a year, and, it being doubtful even then whether the charges brought against him amounted to treason, the odious old contrivance of the worst kings was resorted to, and a bill of attainder was brought in against him. He was a violently prejudiced and mischievous person; had had strong ear-cropping and nose-splitting propensities, as you know; and had done a world of harm. But he dicd peaceably, and like a brave old man.

When the Parliament had got the King into their hands, they became very anxious to get rid of their army, in which Oliver Cromwell had begun to acquire great power; not only because of his courage and high abilities, but because he professed to be very sincere in the Scottish sort of Puritan religion that was then exceedingly popular among the soldiers. They were as much opposed to the Bishops as to the Pope himself; and the very privates, drummers, and trumpeters, had such an inconvenient habit of starting up and preaching long-winded discourses, that I would not have belonged to that army on any account.

So, the Parliament, being far from sure but that the army might begin to preach and fight against them now it had nothing else to do, proposed to disband the greater part of it, to send another part to serve in Ireland against the rebels, and to keep only a small force in England. But, the army would not consent to be broken up, except upon its own conditions; and, when the Parliament showed an intention of compelling it, it acted for itself in an unexpected manner. A certain cornet, of the name of JOICE, arrived at Holmby House one night, attended by four hundred horsemen, went into the King's room with his hat in one hand and a pistol in the other, and told the King that he had come to take him away. The King was willing enough to go, and only stipulated that he should be publicly required to do so next morning. Next morning, accordingly, he appeared on the top of the steps of the house, and asked Cornet Joice before his men and the guard set there by the Parliament, what authority he had for taking him away? To this Cornet Joice replied, 'The authority of the army.' 'Have you a written commission?' said the King. Joice, pointing to his four hundred men on horseback, replied, 'That is my commission.' 'Well,' said the King, smiling, as if he were pleased, 'I never before read such a commission; but it is written in fair and legible characters. This is a company of as handsome proper gentlemen as I have seen a long while.' He was asked where he would like to live, and he said at Newmarket. So, to Newmarket he and Cornet Joice and the four hundred horsemen rode; the King remarking, in the same smiling way, that he could ride as far at a spell as Cornet Joice, or any man there.

The King quite believed, I think, that the army were his friends. He said as much to Fairfax when that general, Oliver Cromwell, and Ireton, went to persuade him to return to the custody of the Parliament. He preferred to remain as he was, and resolved to remain as he was. And when the army moved nearer and nearer London to frighten the Parliament into yielding to their demands, they took the King with them. It was a deplorable thing that England should be at the mercy of a great body of soldiers with arms in their hands; but the King certainly favoured them at this important time of his life, as compared with the more lawful power that tried to control him. It must be added, however, that they treated him, as yet, more respectfully and kindly than the Parliament had done. They allowed him to be attended by his own servants, to be splendidly entertained at various houses, and to see his children—at Cavesham House, near Reading—for two days. Whereas, the Parliament had been rather hard with him, and had only allowed him to ride out and play at bowls.

It is much to be believed that if the King could have been trusted, even at this time, he might have been saved. Even Oliver Cromwell expressly said that he did believe that no man could enjoy his possessions in peace, unless the King had his rights. He was not unfriendly toward the King; he had been present when he received his children, and had been much affected by the pitiable nature of the scene; he saw the King often; he frequently walked and talked with him in the long galleries and pleasant gardens of the Palace at Hampton Court, whither he was now removed; and in all this risked something of his influence with the army. But, the King was in secret hopes of help from the Scottish people; and the moment he was encouraged to join them he began to be cool to his new friends, the army, and to tell the officers that they could not possibly do without him. At the very time, too, when he was promising to make Cromwell and Ireton noblemen, if they would help him up to his old height, he was writing to the Queen that he meant to hang them. They both afterwards declared that they had been privately informed that such a letter would be found, on a certain evening, sewed up in a saddle which would be taken to the Blue Boar in Holborn to be sent to Dover; and that they went there, disguised as common soldiers, and sat drinking in the inn-yard until a man came with the saddle, which they ripped up with their knives, and therein found the letter. I see little reason to doubt the story. It is certain that Oliver Cromwell told one of the King's most faithful followers that the King could not be trusted, and that he would not be answerable if anything amiss were to happen to him. Still, even after that, he kept a promise he had made to the King, by letting him know that there was a plot with a certain portion of the army to seize him. I believe that, in fact, he sincerely wanted the King to escape abroad, and so to be got rid of without more trouble or danger. That Oliver himself had work enough with the army is pretty plain; for some of the troops were so mutinous against him, and against those who acted with him at this time, that he found it necessary to have one man shot at the head of his regiment to overawe the rest.

The King, when he received Oliver's warning, made his escape from Hampton Court; after some indecision and uncertainty, he went to Carisbrooke Castle in the Isle of Wight. At first, he was pretty free there; but, even there, he carried on a pretended treaty with the Parliament, while he was really treating with commissioners from Scotland to send an army into England to take his part. When he broke off this treaty with the Parliament (having settled with Scotland) and was treated as a prisoner, his treatment was not changed too soon, for he had plotted to escape that very night to a ship sent by the Queen, which was lying off the island.

He was doomed to be disappointed in his hopes from Scotland. The agreement he had made with the Scottish Commissioners was not favourable enough to the religion of that country to please the Scottish clergy; and they preached against it. The consequence was, that the army raised in Scotland and sent over, was too small to do much; and that, although it was helped by a rising of the Royalists in England and by good soldiers from Ireland, it could make no head against the Parliamentary army under such men as Cromwell and Fairfax. The King's eldest son, the Prince of Wales, came over from Holland with nineteen ships (a part of the English fleet having gone over to him) to help his father; but nothing came of his voyage, and he was fain to return. The most remarkable event of this second civil war was the cruel execution by the Parliamentary General, of SIR CHARLES LUCAS and SIR GEORGE LISLE, two grand Royalist generals, who had bravely defended Colchester under every disadvantage of famine and distress for nearly three months. When Sir Charles Lucas was shot, Sir George Lisle kissed his body, and said to the soldiers who were to shoot him, 'Come nearer, and make sure of me.' 'I warrant you, Sir George,' said one of the soldiers, 'we shall hit you.' 'Ay?' he returned with a smile, 'but I have been nearer to you, my friends, many a time, and you have missed me.'

The Parliament, after being fearfully bullied by the army—who demanded to have seven members whom they disliked given up to them—had voted that they would have nothing more to do with the King. On the conclusion, however, of this second civil war (which did not last more than six months), they appointed commissioners to treat with him. The King, then so far released again as to be allowed to live in a private house at Newport in the Isle of Wight, managed his own part of the negotiation with a sense that was admired by all who saw him, and gave up, in the end, all that was asked of him—even yielding (which he had steadily refused, so far) to the temporary abolition of the bishops, and the transfer of their church land to the Crown. Still, with his old fatal vice upon him, when his best friends joined the commissioners in beseeching him to yield all those points as the only means of saving himself from the army, he was plotting to escape from the island; he was holding correspondence with his friends and the Catholics in Ireland, though declaring that he was not; and he was writing, with his own hand, that in what he yielded he meant nothing but to get time to escape.

Matters were at this pass when the army, resolved to defy the Parliament, marched up to London. The Parliament, not afraid of them now, and boldly led by Hollis, voted that the King's concessions were sufficient ground for settling the peace of the kingdom. Upon that, COLONEL RICH and COLONEL PRIDE went down to the House of Commons with a regiment of horse soldiers and a regiment of foot; and Colonel Pride, standing in the lobby with a list of the members who were obnoxious to the army in his hand, had them pointed out to him as they came through, and took them all into custody. This proceeding was afterwards called by the people, for a joke, PRIDE'S PURGE. Cromwell was in the North, at the head of his men, at the time, but when he came home, approved of what had been done.

What with imprisoning some members and causing others to stay away, the army had now reduced the House of Commons to some fifty or so. These soon voted that it was treason in a king to make war against his parliament and his people, and sent an ordinance up to the House of Lords for the King's being tried as a traitor. The House of Lords, then sixteen in number, to a man rejected it. Thereupon, the Commons made an ordinance of their own, that they were the supreme government of the country, and would bring the King to trial.

The King had been taken for security to a place called Hurst Castle: a lonely house on a rock in the sea, connected with the coast of Hampshire by a rough road two miles long at low water. Thence, he was ordered to be removed to Windsor; thence, after being but rudely used there, and having none but soldiers to wait upon him at table, he was brought up to St James's Palace in London, and told that his trial was appointed for next day.

On Saturday, the twentieth of January, one thousand six hundred and forty-nine, this memorable trial began. The House of Commons had settled that one hundred and thirty-five persons should form the Court, and these were taken from the House itself, from among the officers of the army, and from among the lawyers and citizens. JOHN BRADSHAW, serjeant-at-law, was appointed president. The place was Westminster Hall. At the upper end, in a red velvet chair, sat the president, with his hat (lined with plates of iron for his protection) on his head. The rest of the Court sat on side benches, also wearing their hats. The King's seat was covered with velvet, like that of the president, and was opposite to it. He was brought from St James's to Whitehall, and from Whitehall he came by water to his trial.

When he came in, he looked round very steadily on the Court, and on the great number of spectators, and then sat down: presently he got up and looked round again. On the indictment 'against Charles Stuart, for high treason,' being read, he smiled several times, and he denied the authority of the Court, saying that there could be no parliament without a House of Lords, and that he saw no House of Lords there. Also, that the King ought to be there, and that he saw no King in the King's right place. Bradshaw replied, that the Court was satisfied with its authority, and that its authority was God's authority and the kingdom's. He then adjourned the Court to the following Monday. On that day, the trial was resumed, and went on all the week. When the Saturday came, as the King passed forward to his place in the Hall, some soldiers and others cried for 'justice!' and execution on him. That day, too, Bradshaw, like an angry Sultan, wore a red robe, instead of the black robe he had worn before. The King was sentenced to death that day. As he went out, one solitary soldier said, 'God bless you, Sir!' For this, his officer struck him. The King said he thought the punishment exceeded the offence. The silver head of his walking-stick had fallen off while he leaned upon it, at one time of the trial. The accident seemed to disturb him, as if he thought it ominous of the falling of his own head; and he admitted as much, now it was all over.

Being taken back to Whitehall, he sent to the House of Commons, saying that as the time of his execution might be nigh, he wished he might be allowed to see his darling children. It was granted. On the Monday he was taken back to St James's; and his two children then in England, the PRINCESS ELIZABETH thirteen years old, and the DUKE OF GLOUCESTER nine years old, were brought to take leave of him, from Sion House, near Brentford. It was a sad and touching scene, when he kissed and fondled those poor children, and made a little present of two diamond seals to the Princess, and gave them tender messages to their mother (who little deserved them, for she had a lover of her own whom she married soon afterwards), and told them that he died 'for the laws and liberties of the land.' I am bound to say that I don't think he did, but I dare say he believed so.

There were ambassadors from Holland that day, to intercede for the unhappy King, whom you and I both wish the Parliament had spared; but they got no answer. The Scottish Commissioners interceded too; so did the Prince of Wales, by a letter in which he offered as the next heir to the throne, to accept any conditions from the

Parliament; so did the Queen, by letter likewise. Notwithstanding all, the warrant for the execution was this day signed. There is a story that as Oliver Cromwell went to the table with the pen in his hand to put his signature to it, he drew his pen across the face of one of the commissioners, who was standing near, and marked it with ink. That commissioner had not signed his own name yet, and the story adds that when he came to do it he marked Cromwell's face with ink in the same way.

The King slept well, untroubled by the knowledge that it was his last night on earth, and rose on the thirtieth of January, two hours before day, and dressed himself carefully. He put on two shirts lest he should tremble with the cold, and had his hair very carefully combed. The warrant had been directed to three officers of the army, COLONEL HACKER, COLONEL HUNKS, and COLONEL PHAYER. At ten o'clock, the first of these came to the door and said it was time to go to Whitehall. The King, who had always been a quick walker, walked at his usual speed through the Park, and called out to the guard, with his accustomed voice of command, 'March on apace!' When he came to Whitehall, he was taken to his own bedroom, where a breakfast was set forth. As he had taken the Sacrament, he would eat nothing more; but, at about the time when the church bells struck twelve at noon (for he had to wait, through the scaffold not being ready), he took the advice of the good BISHOP JUXON who was with him, and ate a little bread and drank a glass of claret. Soon after he had taken this refreshment, Colonel Hacker came to the chamber with the warrant in his hand, and called for Charles Stuart.

And then, through the long gallery of Whitehall Palace, which he had often seen light and gay and merry and crowded, in very different times, the fallen King passed along, until he came to the centre window of the Banqueting House, through which he emerged upon the scaffold, which was hung with black. He looked at the two executioners, who were dressed in black and masked; he looked at the troops of soldiers on horseback and on foot, and all looked up at him in silence; he looked at the vast array of spectators, filling up the view beyond, and turning all their faces upon him; he looked at his old Palace of St James's; and he looked at the block. He seemed a little troubled to find that it was so low, and asked, 'if there were no place higher?' Then, to those upon the scaffold, he said, 'that it was the Parliament who had begun the war, and not he; but he hoped they might be guiltless too, as ill instruments had gone between them. In one respect,' he said, 'he suffered justly; and that was because he had permitted an unjust sentence to be executed on another.' In this he referred to the Earl of Strafford.

He was not at all afraid to die; but he was anxious to die easily. When some one touched the axe while he was speaking, he broke off and called out, 'Take heed of the axe! take heed of the axe!' He also said to Colonel Hacker, 'Take care that they do not put me to pain.' He told the executioners, 'I shall say but very short prayers, and then thrust out my hands'—as the sign to strike.

He put his hair up, under a white satin cap which the bishop had carried, and said, 'I have a good cause and a gracious God on my side.' The bishop told him that he had but one stage more to travel in this weary world, and that, though it was a turbulent and troublesome stage, it was a short one, and would carry him a great way—all the way from earth to Heaven. The King's last word, as he gave his cloak and the George—the decoration from his breast—to the bishop, was, 'Remember!' He then kneeled down, laid his head on the block, spread out his hands, and was instantly killed. One universal groan broke from the crowd; and the soldiers, who had sat on their horses and stood in their ranks immovable as statues, were of a sudden all in motion, clearing the streets.

Thus, in the forty-ninth year of his age, falling at the same time of his career as Strafford had fallen in his, perished Charles the First. With all my sorrow for him, I cannot agree with him that he died 'the martyr of the people'; for the people had been martyrs to him, and to his ideas of a King's rights, long before. Indeed, I am afraid that he was but a bad judge of martyrs; for he had called that infamous Duke of Buckingham 'the Martyr of his Sovereign.'